HOW TO BECOME A
ROCK STAR CHEF

Praise for *How to Become a Rock Star Chef*

With *How To Become A Rock Star Chef*, Chef Mark Garcia masterfully combines all the right ingredients to show you how to supercharge your brand in the New Digital economy. Uniquely profound in its understanding of the boardroom and the kitchen, this book is a must read for anyone interested in making their culinary venture a success."

—**Kevin Hartman**, Head of Industry, Google

"A must read for any chef who aspires to be relevant on the national stage. Chef Garcia packages over a decade of international digital experience with the world's best & brightest with one of the most aggressive programs in the food industry and provides actionable insights that are "must-haves". The first author with the dual-discipline background and Fortune 500 experience to bridge the Culinary-Digital divide. If your food is phenomenal but you can't reach that next level, Chef Garcia provides the missing pieces that are critical to elevating *"Great"* chefs to *"Rock Star"* status.

—**Gary Freeman**, Principal, MIDAS Foods International

"Strategic branding, marketing and positioning is the defining business model of our day, and *How To Become A Rock Star Chef* captures the essence of this emerging model and shows chefs and restaurateurs how to apply it in the New Digital Economy. Those who want to differentiate and find new ways to grow their business and increase profits should find this book extremely helpful."

—**Merri Kingsly**, Founder and CEO, ML Kingsly & Associates, Former Publisher, SAVEUR Magazine

"Chef Mark Garcia has taken a topic close to the hearts of many—digital media—in a global industry, culinary, and shown how the world's leading companies have successfully integrated it into their business models. *How To Become A Rock Star Chef* is that rare book which will help unify the disparate parts of a big company, from marketing to sales to product development."

—**Thomas Keslinke**, CEO, Chef's Roll, Inc.

"Mark Garcia doesn't just know how to create mega-success. He knows how to inspire people to make it happen for themselves. This book is equal parts mini marketing MBA and high-amp motivational pep-talk. It will give you the tools you need to turn yourself into a revenue-generating brand—and the kick in the pants you need to start that career transformation today."

—**Steve Siegelman**, Executive Creative Director, Ketchum Inc.

Also by Mark Garcia
Entrepreneurial Insanity in the Restaurant Business
The 7-Step Recipe for Social Media Success

Seminars by Chef Mark Garcia
Rock Star Chef Marketing Academy
7-Step Recipe For Social Media Success
High-Performance Habits of Multimillionaires

Meet Mark online and receive free training at
www.ChefMarkGarcia.com

HOW TO BECOME A
ROCK STAR CHEF

11 STEPS TO DOMINATE YOUR MARKET
IN THE NEW DIGITAL ECONOMY

Chef Mark Garcia

Founder of Rock Star Chef Marketing Academy

NEW YORK

NASHVILLE • MELBOURNE • VANCOUVER

HOW TO BECOME A ROCK STAR CHEF
11 STEPS TO DOMINATE YOUR MARKET IN THE NEW DIGITAL ECONOMY

© 2018 **Chef Mark Garcia**

Published in New York, New York, by Morgan James Publishing. Morgan James is a trademark of Morgan James, LLC. www.MorganJamesPublishing.com

The Morgan James Speakers Group can bring authors to your live event. For more information or to book an event visit The Morgan James Speakers Group at www.TheMorganJamesSpeakersGroup.com.

ISBN 978-1-63047-101-9 paperback
ISBN 978-1-63047-102-6 eBook
ISBN 978-1-63047-103-3 hardcover
Library of Congress Control Number: 2014933725

In an effort to support local communities, raise awareness and funds, Morgan James Publishing donates a percentage of all book sales for the life of each book to Habitat for Humanity Peninsula and Greater Williamsburg.

Get involved today! Visit
www.MorganJamesBuilds.com

To my daughter, Alexis Garcia, whose mere presence in my life has challenged me daily to be the best man, the best father, the best provider and the best friend I can be. Becoming a parent made me become a more mature adult, becoming your Daddy made me become a better man. I cherish every moment with you. My wish is that this book will remind you of your own unlimited potential and Rock Star status…

I love you, princess.

Daddy

TABLE OF CONTENTS

WHAT IS A ROCK STAR CHEF?

ROCK STAR

Main Entry: Rock Star

Pronunciation: \'rok\ \'star\

Function: Noun

Origin: Late twentieth century

Definition: A famous singer of rock music. Someone who is in a popular rock band. A person who doesn't always follow the rules—they make their own. They go out of their way to be extraordinary and unique. Someone who lives a lifestyle that others only dream of. Master of a particular domain, who is true to oneself and one's very nature, living without limitations or restrictions. A trailblazer or maverick that holds a unique position or level of status within the marketplace. One who is famous by using one's life skills or other talents to define an industry.

—Urban Dictionary

CHEF

Main Entry: Chef

Pronunciation: \'shef\

Function: Noun, Intransitive Verb

Origin: 1840. French, short for *chef de cuisine* (chief or head of the kitchen)

Definition: A skilled cook who manages the kitchen in a restaurant or hotel. A cook, especially in a skilled or professional capacity. The chief cook, usually responsible for planning menus, ordering foodstuffs, overseeing food preparation, and supervising the kitchen staff. A person who prepares food by some manner of heating.

Synonyms: chef, cooker, culinarian

—Merriam-Webster's Online Dictionary

FOREWORD

In an era of rampant change, few things have evolved more than how
and what we eat. All of us can tell this tale through the lens of our
own experience, but the story is invariably the same. For me, growing
up in Cincinnati in the 1970s, there was one great restaurant—a
French one, the Maisonette, God rest its Gallic soul—a few merely
good ones, and a lot of fast-food chains and coffee shops. There were
interesting local options, such as the acquired taste of Skyline chili
or the deservedly famous Graeter's ice cream. An ethnic meal meant
Chinese food, which meant egg rolls, chow mein, and egg foo young.
Not a sushi joint be found within 100 miles, much less Thai or
Indian or Mexican (and no, Chi Chi's didn't count as Mexican). Rock
Star Chefs? Not so much. Perhaps the only celebrity chef of the day
was Julia, that early master of omnichannel media in an otherwise
analog age.

I moved to New York City in 1987. Compared to Cincinnati in
the seventies, New York in the go-go eighties was a veritable bounty
of good to great to sublime food options. Every ethnic cuisine under
the sun was represented, universally made by natives mostly cooking

for other natives. Of course, New York City was legendary for pizza joints and Jewish delis and Greek diners. In the world of fine dining, trailblazers like Danny Meyer (Union Square Café) and Alfred Portale (Gotham Bar and Grill) were redefining American cuisine. Places like Le Bernardin and Bouley were battling for top ranking in the annual Zagat survey. In fact, haute French cuisine dominated the four-star rankings of the *New York Times:* Lutece, La Grenouille, Le Cirque, and La Caravelle. If, like me, you were food-obsessed at the time, you knew the names of the chefs at all these places. Maybe you got to see them strolling around the dining room on occasion. But rock stars they were not—and hardly known outside New York, except among the small community of global food cognoscenti who also knew about Puck, Waters, Robuchon, and Ducasse.

Downtown, a couple of young upstarts were about to change the game. Sometime during the first few years of my life in Manhattan, Bobby Flay opened Miracle Grill, and Mario Batali opened Po. While their restaurants were great, fun places to eat, these two guys, along with Emeril Lagasse, were about to hit the jackpot of all jackpots of talent, timing, and telegenics. A massive media convergence was beginning to take shape. This media "big bang" would eventually give rise to a new constellation: the Rock Star Chefs. It combined cookbooks and 24-hour dedicated cable television programming with early digital media and e-commerce and, eventually, social media and smartphones and tablets. It spread from restaurants to kitchens to a myriad of social movements such as organic and locavore and farm-to-table. And, like the very stars in the heavens, this universe is always on.

The road to rock stardom was paved with massive changes in media, technology, demographics, and consumer lifestyles. Bobby, Mario, and Emeril were the first ones to get on the tour bus, but others soon followed. The cookbooks and cable shows set the stage for growing restaurant empires, garnering more and more exposure, fans, and groupies. Soon after, social media came along to add more fuel to the fire. Today's biggest Rock Star Chefs, such as Anthony Bourdain and Jamie Oliver, count their Twitter followers in the millions—far more than all but a few music stars.

Rock Star Chefs are now household names—brands unto themselves, capable of moving everything from books to grocery products to housewares and, of course, restaurant reservations. A new recipe had been created: start with a heaping measure of talent, whisk in a boiling pot of chutzpah, and blend it all together on high speed with continuous pinches of technology and social connection. You'll end up with a delicious dish of convergence beyond the wildest imagination of even our dear, beloved Julia.

Mark Garcia's got the bead on this new recipe. In fact, he helped write it! If you've ever dreamt of being a Rock Star Chef, this is now your cookbook. He's uncovered every secret, every trick of the trade, for finding fame and fortune with your kitchen talents. Never has the toolbox been bigger or the canvas broader. But still, you need someone to show you how to swing the hammer and move the brush. Let Mark be your guide.

I first met Mark in 2011 when my digital agency, R/GA, began working with Mark's client, McCormick, the global giant in flavors and spices. I saw firsthand how Mark bridged his talent for cooking with his nose for business and his love of technology and media. This book is the intersection of those passions.

In my opinion, the Rock Star Chefs arrived just in time. Right as the world of musical rock stars was going down the black hole of history, the universe gave birth to an entire new species of stars who make their music in a different kitchen. And, since all of us eat every day, we likely consume far more of the fruits of their labor than we ever did of Mick or Keith or John or Paul or Jimi.

No doubt, it's good to be a Rock Star Chef.

—**Barry Wacksman**, EVP and Global Chief Growth Officer, R/GA, New York City, Bestselling Author of *Connected By Design: 7 Principles for Business Transformation Through Functional Integration*

INTRODUCTION

"One can never know too much; the more one learns, the more one sees the need to learn more and that study, as well as broadening the mind of the craftsman, provides an easy way of perfecting yourself in the practice of your art."

—**Auguste Escoffier**

Are you ready to bump your business up to the next level in revenue? Are you a chef looking to boost your profile and get a cookbook deal, open your own joint, or have your very own cooking show? Are you ready to be instantly recognizable? If your answer to any of these questions is an unequivocal, enthusiastic "YES!" then read the following list:

Wolfgang Puck, Eric Ripert, Emeril Lagasse, Paul Bocuse, Charlie Trotter, Grant Achatz, Scott Conant, John Besh, Dean Fearing, Aaron Sanchez, Kent Rathbun, Stephen Pyles, David Burke, David Change, Todd English, Jöel Robuchon, Ferran Adrià, Anthony Bourdain, José Andrés, Bobby Flay, Alain Ducasse, Daniel Boloud, Mario Batali, Paul Qui, Guy Fieri, Gordon Ramsay, Jamie Oliver, Ming Tsai, Paula Deen, or Rachel Ray. Okay, what images come up in your mind when you read those names?

You may be asking yourself what these famous people all have in common. I mention these names because every one of them is much more than just a chef of rock star fame, a TV personality, or a restaurateur. Each of them is a *brand* unto him- or herself. From Wolfgang Puck, with his stable of restaurants, frozen-food concepts, cookware, and high-profile catering gigs, to Rachel Ray, with her almost overnight stratospheric career launch from supermarket demo chef to Food Network megastar, cookbook author, lifestyle daytime show and magazine owner, pop culture celebrity, and overall cooking diva, they each have etched their brand indelibly into the consciousness of society today and have built million-dollar empires in the process.

Every Rock Star Chef on this page has built a platform from which they can influence the world of food, and they have thousands, if not millions, of fans all over the globe. They have figured out how to be famous and recognizable around the world—by mastering the art and science of strategic marketing, branding, and licensing. Some have their own cooking show, while others are starring in a big-budget Hollywood movie, selling their latest wares on one of the home-shopping TV channels, or licensing their name and logo on hundreds of products. It is reported that Emeril Lagasse has over 753 licensing agreements alone!

Each of these maverick marketing masters has figured out how to rise above the noise of the wannabes and become an ultra successful ROCK STAR CHEF!

And I'm willing to bet that not one of them has a fancy MBA in marketing from the Wharton School of Business or Harvard Business School. I would also be willing to bet that not one of them was born with a silver spoon in their mouth, a trust fund, or a pedigree from a long lineage of European nobility such as Rothschild, DeBeers, or Windsor.

They've never run a Fortune 500 company—or, for that matter, any company that had more than a couple of hundred employees. I think it's safe to say that most of these people had very humble beginnings and had to work their **ass**ets off to get where they are now.

By the way, where do you think these entrepreneurially minded chefs and restaurateurs might have learned how a *true* rock star brands, promotes, licenses, and markets himself? I'm pretty sure that whatever your age, you have heard of the rock band KISS and its cofounder Gene Simmons. Besides enjoying close to forty years of success with the band (they continue to sell out stadiums all over the world), millions of records sold, and a long-running reality TV show, Gene has built a licensing empire that any Fortune 500 company or world-class athlete would be envious of. To date, he has over 2,500 licensing and royalty deals! And you've gotta give props to the guy who also had the insight to register the trademark for "OJ" (the drink, not the fallen football star).

So why am I telling you to study the example of these individuals and learn from their trailblazing careers? Think about what each one of them has accomplished in a fairly short time. Every one of these individuals rose from nameless obscurity to become an icon in their particular arena of the food-and-beverage world. Most of these juggernauts are recognizable by just one name: "Wolfgang," "Emeril," "Flay," "Ripert" (that's *Ree-pair*), "Rachel," and "Bocuse." Who doesn't know precisely whom you are referring to when you mention "Ramsey" or "Keller"?

All these Rock Star Chefs became wildly successful in the culinary world because they blazed their own trail. Of course they worked hard, but they also worked *smart*! They didn't just plod along the traditional pathways of doing business.

No, they made their own rules as they went along and, in the process, developed major success and worldwide celebrity. In life, success comes to the confident, the bold, and the aggressive. By being unique, strategically positioning their brand and creatively marketing outside the box, they had large consumer product corporations (CPG's), kitchen equipment companies, TV networks, publishers, hotel groups, investors, and marketing companies beating a path to their door and showering them with money and contracts.

And isn't that exactly what *you* want to accomplish in your professional life or business? Maybe you already own a restaurant and you're trying to attract investors to grow into multiple locations or concepts.

Do you want your restaurant to be known as *"the"* hot spot in town? Imagine the envy your competition will feel as their customers and their dollars drive right past their half-empty parking lots on the way to your filled-to-capacity dining room.

When a news story breaks in your industry, or a reporter is looking to interview an expert to comment on recent trends, don't you want to be the one they go to for an opinion? That is what the Rock Star Chef Marketing System is all about! It's about learning the tricks of the trade. (Or *trucs,* for my fellow Frenchmen!) It's about learning how to market effectively both online and offline. It's about learning how to build your brand and position yourself or your business to stand out from the crowd. In these pages, you will quickly learn the fastest way to build your personal brand, celebrity chef persona, and mystique.

That's where I come in. I am going to guide you through the marketing maze on the journey to becoming a Rock Star Chef or a Rock Star Restaurateur. What do I know about being a rock star or a chef? Plenty! I played bass guitar professionally on the music scene during the mid- to late 1980s in Phoenix and Los Angeles. If you recall, this was during the time of the "glam metal" or "hair band" scene.

Bands like Poison, Ratt, Mötley Crüe, Guns n' Roses, WASP, Quiet Riot, Warrant, L.A. Guns, Metallica, and others were all slugging it out trying to get signed to a record deal and become the next "it" group. The way these hungry bands got the word out about their next gig was by pure guerrilla street-marketing tactics. They didn't have an expensive PR agent or a large marketing department. Hell, most of them had no money and were surviving on money given to them by band groupies from the L.A. music scene. Every band member became a tireless self-promoting machine—posting flyers, networking, and doing anything else they possibly could (legal and maybe not so legal) to get their band's name on minds and lips all over town.

You see, the way the game was played back in the day was that almost every concert venue that would book these bands charged an "up-front fee" to play. That's right, just about every L.A. band you know of that got famous around then had to pay for the privilege to go onstage in the beginning of their career. No bar owner was going to take a chance on an unknown band, and they sure as hell weren't going to pay them ANY money. So if you wanted to play Gazzari's, the Whiskey, the Troubadour, or any of the other clubs, you had to pay (cash, of course) several thousand dollars for your set.

If you wanted to make your money back—which you desperately did so that you could pay rent, eat, or pay off the local "small business loan associate" you borrowed the money from—you had to sell enough tickets to your show. Otherwise, if nobody showed up when your gig was scheduled, tough!

Now, do you think you might learn how to hustle and flow to get the word out about your band if you were ponying up money that you didn't have just for the chance to play in front of people? That would be like a chef having to go to a restaurant owner, beg for a night of the week to cook, pay for all the food up front, and then market like hell to get people to come in and eat.

One aspect of the music business that always intrigued me was the concept of residual income and royalties or, as I like to call it,

Mailbox Money

Here's what I mean. When you write, compose, produce, or create a song you have publishing rights. If you get that song or album on the market and have actual sales of the material, you now have royalties, or residuals, every time your song is played on the radio, purchased at a store, part of a film soundtrack, downloaded on iTunes, featured in a soundtrack, used in a video game or slot machine, used in a commercial, or played on a Muzak track. That is to say, YOU GET PAID! Do the work once and get paid for it over and over again—even while you sleep. Think about that for a second. There are bands and recording artists who have been getting checks in their mailbox every month for years—decades, even! Some of them have passed away, and their estates are still getting this mailbox money.

By the way, this income is recognized and taxed much differently from the money you earn as straight income from a job. But that's a topic for another book. Let's just say that when I understood the power of the concept of residual income, I promised myself I would figure out how to make that happen in my life. Later in this book, I'll discuss how, in the new digital economy, it is actually *more* achievable and realistic to implement than ever before.

As an award-winning professional chef, I have worked in Five-Star restaurants and Five-Diamond hotels both here in the States and in Europe. When I was cooking in some of the most prestigious and famous New York City restaurants, all the studio musicians and we chefs worked similar hours and hung out at the same after-hours clubs. We were kindred spirits and shared the same creative passion for our crafts. We also shared the same interests in members of the opposite sex who loved musicians and chefs, but that is a "whole 'nother subject for a tell-all book.

So why am I presuming to tell you what it means to be a Rock Star Chef? For starters, I am an honors graduate of the Culinary Institute of America (CIA) and was awarded a teaching fellowship at this prestigious school right after graduation. It has been called the Harvard of cooking schools, and its faculty and graduates are some of the most influential pioneers in the cooking world. And yes, many of the graduates are also the winners of just about every major reality chef competition on television these days.

The consulting agency I opened over fifteen years ago has worked with some of the largest corporations in the world. I have also been blessed to work personally with five different billionaires (yes, that's with a "b") from the restaurant, NFL team ownership, and gourmet grocery retail worlds. These superstars taught me many lessons in business and finance, but the greatest lesson they inspired me with was the importance of *servant leadership* and how to be a great contributor to the world instead of just being a consumer. Jonathan, Danny, Charles, Red, and Phil, I thank you every day of my life for your wisdom and your stellar example.

With my Fortune 500 clients and job assignments, I have created recipes, brick-and-mortar concepts, and food items for several major restaurant, manufacturing, retail, food service, and hotel companies. Heck, I've even been part of the small team responsible for not one, but two different Super Bowl commercials and campaigns. For any marketer, ad agency or creative, to work on a Super Bowl campaign is considered **the** "Holy Grail" of advertising. Millions of dollars and billions of media impressions are at stake. I have been truly blessed in my career to have worked with some of the biggest and most respected brands in the world.

Companies such as McCormick, Brinker International, Darden Restaurants, Avocados From Mexico, Wegmans, Central Market, Whole Foods, Trader Joe's, Sam's Club, Jack Daniels, Tyson, Wal-Mart, Costco, Safeway, Publix, Sofitel, and Ritz Carlton Hotels have all benefited from my experience, insight, and knowledge. I have people paying thousands of dollars to come to my seminars; I have coaching and consulting clients who pay me tens of thousands of dollars per year. I have multimillion-dollar product launches for gourmet retailers, as well as celebrity chefs, musicians, beverage companies and sports star clients under my belt.

I have also worked with many of the celebrity chefs that you see on Food Network or other cooking shows such as *Top Chef, Chopped, Iron Chef, Hell's Kitchen,* and many others. As a matter of fact, if you are reading this book, there is a 95 percent chance that you have eaten a meal or recipe that I had a hand in creating. I tell you these things not to wow you and impress you, but to share with you as real-world examples, so you'll know that I know what I'm talking about. I've been doing this for almost two decades—it's not just theory for me. Believe me, I have had more failures and product duds than I care to remember. The beauty of it for you is that you get to shorten your learning curve by learning from my mistakes *and* my successes.

As a marketer and brand executive in the New Digital economy, I oversee the creation, delivery, and execution of many groundbreaking digital, mobile, and social media platforms. We have responsibility for multiple marketing, brand and strategy campaigns that cost tens of millions of dollars to produce and execute. Many of these programs have won industry awards and media recognition as unique, innovative, cutting-edge campaigns.

While the industry recognition and awards are great—and who of us doesn't like to be acknowledged for our good work?—The better gauge of success for me was the bottom-line impact that all this work did for the businesses or brands associated with these campaigns.

The principles I have honed and perfected over the years are what I am going to teach you in this program. To reach people now takes an enormous degree of intelligence, relevance, and value. Listen—I struggled for many years trying to figure out how to do the things I do. I would implement something, test the results, tweak things a bit, and start the whole process over again. If I didn't know how to do something online, I either hired someone to teach me or just rolled up my sleeves and figured it out! There at the beginning, I made more mistakes than anyone can imagine. But I learned from those mistakes and quickly achieved levels of success that I once only dreamed of.

When I first started my own company, there were many lean times in the beginning. As a matter of fact, I often lay awake at night, worried to death about how I was going to pay the mortgage for the next month. At the time, as a newly single father with a young daughter under my full time care, I was motivated to achieve real results and gain customers fast!

You get to benefit from all those hard lessons I learned, and your path to success will be much quicker than mine was. I wish I had had someone to guide me and teach me the shortcuts early in my career. I could have shaved *years* off my learning curve and achieved success so much faster.

In this book, I am going to lay out, step by step, exactly how and why you need to build YOUR personal brand. Yes, that's true even if you currently work for someone else's restaurant or even a large corporation. Make no mistake about it: as an employee, too, if you want to stay relevant and competitive in the coming years, you will need to develop and grow your personal brand.

Everyone needs to wrap their mind-set around the fact that they MUST start thinking of themselves as a brand. No exceptions—not anymore. It's an absolute necessity.

I think you would agree with me that the Internet represents one of the biggest cultural shifts since Gutenberg's movable-type printing press. In this book and in my programs, you will learn to harness the power of the Internet and social media in this most unprecedented time in human history.

Those wise enough to take advantage of this window of opportunity that is now open will reap rewards beyond belief. I believe that most of society and—get this—*especially* corporate America has been slow to recognize that this shift also represents a radically different way that we conduct business or engage in business-to-consumer (B2C) relationships.

This is so because, now more than ever, you as an individual have the combined arsenal of tools, bandwidth, and capabilities to reach millions of fans in ways that were unheard-of just a few years ago. The playing field has been leveled, and you can now go toe-to-toe against the large corporations and their million-dollar PR budgets. Hell, in some arenas the game has changed so drastically that what we do right now in digital marketing wasn't even *possible* just three short years ago!

Think about that last sentence. The possibilities for smart marketers and those who know how to take advantage of the technology mean they can be game changers in any industry or business arena that they decide to play in.

This is a book about the new era of business, the new influence of customers, the new platforms for internet marketing and your role in defining the future of everything you do in the digital world.

Throughout these upcoming chapters, I will be making **BIG-ASS, BOLD** statements. Rest assured that I don't say these things lightly or in jest. I have pondered, researched, and experienced the data and actions that have led me to the thoughts, predictions, and comments I will be sharing with you.

The World Is Changing Fast. Are You Ready for It?

Old economy versus new economy. Old media versus new media. Traditional advertising versus digital advertising. Chain restaurants across the country versus the local mom-and-pop diner.

Not a day goes by that you don't see an article or hear a news report mentioning the above comparisons. We live in amazing times right now—times ripe with phenomenal business and personal opportunities. The challenge is that most of the old rules don't apply, and in a few weeks, months, or years, the rest of them won't either. The pace of change is *mind-boggling*. Many of us are simply overwhelmed by the rapid flow of information and speed of change that is taking place in both the online and offline worlds. We live in interesting, fascinating, gobsmackingly *amazing* times, and the rate of change we are experiencing right now is nothing less than historic, to put it mildly.

So where are we moving to? What are the trends, opportunities, and new realities for chefs, restaurateurs, and food service professionals in this New Digital economy?

I am going to show you a step-by-step recipe (or path, if you will) on how to **OUTSMART**, **OUTHUSTLE**, **OUTMARKET**, and **OUTBRAND** your competition. With the tools and platforms that exist today, it is possible for you to have the same level of marketing, production, and business success that, up until this time in history, was the sole preserve of multimillion-dollar companies.

If you ever wanted to know how to take your culinary passion, your knowledge, your products or services and build a profitable business around them, then you are in the right place. If you ever wanted to take your years of hard-won knowledge and expertise from the culinary world to the masses and get paid for it, you are in the right place.

Are you interested in becoming a cookbook author? Did you know that the entire publishing world is going through a major shift right now? The opportunity for you to create that book that you always knew you needed to write and publish but didn't know how is totally *within your grasp*! Would it surprise you to know that you could have that book in your hands in as little as thirty days? I have done it, and so have many of my colleagues.

Thanks to the New Digital Economy and companies like Amazon's Print on Demand division, not only is it possible, but hundreds of people are doing it every month. With the rise of e-book readers such as the Kindle Fire and others, more and more authors can now have access to a huge audience and a channel for publishing that didn't exist just a few short years ago!

Have you ever wanted to get your killer recipes sold inside gourmet grocery stores? It's not hard, but it does take hard work, strategic positioning and business smarts. You'll have to know the right manufacturers if you want to create your product safely, efficiently, and at a reasonable price. You will also have to know the right distributors to transport your products quickly and competently, and you will need to know the inside track to the buyers and decision makers at the various retailers. Now, do you want to learn this from someone who has been doing it for years and has multimillion-dollar product lines as proof? Or would you rather learn it from your cousin's neighbor's bingo partner who once sold her hot sauce to a local deli?

Or does having your own cooking show suit your style more? There are many ways to achieve this dream, and there are many platforms where you can broadcast successfully—TV is only *one* of them. We can now create broadcast-quality cooking segments and distribute that content faster and cheaper than ever before in human history.

What about becoming a brand ambassador or celebrity spokesperson for a large company? Did you know that hundreds of large food manufacturers and retail brands hire chefs all the time to be their highly paid mouthpieces? Or does the title "culinary consultant" resonate more with you? Restaurant, retail, manufacturing and hotel companies are searching for these types of individuals every day of every week of every month of every year.

IT IS POSSIBLE. You can do this. I've done it repeatedly, and so have many of my clients. This book is about how to be successful. However I will tell you that I was not truly successful until I decided to also be charitable. I'll share those lessons with you later in this book as well.

Celebrity chefs didn't become that way overnight, and it didn't happen by accident. In fact, most of the people I know will tell you that their "overnight success" took only twelve years or so! Most chefs, restaurateurs, and club owners tell stories of starting at the bottom and plying their craft in the humblest of places. Each one of them will also tell you that during this period they were having the time of their lives. Why? Because they were doing what they loved and what they felt was their calling. There is freedom in realizing your passion.

It takes commitment, hard work and consistent action to become a Rock Star Chef. Nobody is going to hand you the silver spoon— or *whisk,* in this case. You must be willing to look at yourself, your business, and your world in a completely different light. You might even have to do things that take you outside your comfort zone, or things that you never imagined yourself doing. Don't worry, you won't be doing anything illegal or immoral, but I *am* definitely going to stretch your current conception of what is possible.

This book is not intended to be a "one and done" read. My hope is that you mark it up—take notes and highlight the portions that are most relevant to you; then revisit and refer to them frequently. I'm going to give you real-world examples and case studies for you to model for your own business. And I'll go beyond that with audio and video case studies you can access on the accompanying membership site for this book. I've also got additional training videos and resources at the website which you can access here: http://rockstarchefbook.com/member

Throughout this book, you will find many practical digital suggestions. These are designed to help you understand the many online and digital tools that exist. New tools and techniques come out often, so please check my site, RockStarChefBook.com, for the latest information and updates.

Now, let's get cooking!

CHAPTER 1
MIND-SET

"A complete lack of caution is perhaps one of the true signs of a real gourmet; he has not need for it, being filled as he is with God-given and intelligently self-cultivated sense of gastronomical freedom."
—**M.F.K. Fisher**

Setting Up the Kitchen Stage

As chefs and restaurateurs, it's in our DNA—we know instinctively that to be successful, we must be extremely organized and detail oriented in our craft. Efficiency and purpose-driven movement are the basics for kitchen success. For if we want any venture to be successful, we must **THINK**, **PLAN**, and **ACT**. Well, the road to becoming a Rock Star Chef is no different from any other work you've done in the kitchen.

Just as you have organized your menu and cooking station for the next dinner service, I'm going to lay out a detailed set of steps that will enable you to build your personal brand and lay the groundwork to becoming a Rock Star Chef. Just as in any professional kitchen, the

Mise en Place mantra here is going to be *"Plan Your Work, and Work Your Plan."*

The More Things Change, the More They Stay the Same

In the introduction to this book, I mentioned how, since the advent of the Internet and the commercial web, things have rapidly and profoundly changed in our world and society. Those changes herald good news and bad news. The good news is that opportunity for chefs and restaurateurs has never been better. The bad news is that human nature is still human nature, and many will simply not take the time to learn about or embrace changing technology and social habits. DON'T be one of those people.

The other bad news is that you are almost certainly late to the party, so to speak, in having a digital presence on the Internet. The good news is, so is just about everyone else! While I will teach you about the exciting gadgets and tools, it's still going to take a new approach to work planning, content creation, and execution if you want to achieve Rock Star Chef status in the New Digital Economy.

The people who are going to be the winners in this new digital space are those who do the best job of listening to, engaging with, and more importantly SERVING their audience. The losers are going to be the folks who still believe in command and control or who simply view this whole Internet and social media "thingy" as some passing fad, like the hula-hoop and the Pet Rock.

The restaurateurs and chefs who fail in the New Digital Economy are the ones who still believe that the path to success is to keep doing what has always worked in the past—the old *"If it ain't broke, don't bother messing with it"* mentality.

What follows in this chapter is exactly what I did in the beginning of my online career to get the results I was searching for. Do you want to learn how I did it? Would you like to see, step-by-step, how I created the successful businesses that I have? Then do these things! Don't just read over them and think I'm putting them here for filler material. I'll say this once: THERE IS NO FILLER IN THIS BOOK. Every word is there because it's vitally important that you get it.

Vision: Sit Down and Write Yourself a Letter

Having a serious vision for your life, your career or business, or your relationships gives you the power to anticipate or expect what will come to pass. All success begins with clarity. But never forget, it's only a thought until you write it down. You are worth it, aren't you? What is the vision for your life, your business, or your career? Write it down!

Now, you're probably thinking you've heard something like this before. And guess what: you are right! If you've done any self-improvement or goal achievement training, you already know that committing thoughts, ideas, and, more importantly, *deadlines* to paper begins the process of achieving those goals. Besides, we're going to have many tasks that need to be done daily that will help you become a Rock Star Chef. I will cover the Seven-Step Plan in chapter 10. I promise you, the recipe that I'm going to show you in that plan is something you have never seen anywhere else.

Don't overcomplicate this task. Create for yourself three to five short-term or long-term goals or projects and write them down on colorful pieces of paper. Display these goals in a place where you will see them every day. On your desk, on your bathroom mirror, wherever—just make sure that you read them and visualize them every day. When you see the momentum and outcomes of those tasks it encourages your progress.

Write down your goals. Commit to those goals—NO squirming or weasel words like "maybe, possibly, hopefully, etc. Claim 100% responsibility for the outcome, regardless of how it goes. Use fear to push you. Fear is a great indicator of what you SHOULD be doing.

Your high level of commitment will get you noticed. It separates the very successful from those who are just getting by playing it safe.

Raison D'Etre: Don't Tell Me What You Do, Tell Me Why You Do It

Most marketers, corporations, brands or celebrities advertise, position or broadcast *"what"* they do. They flood the marketplace with their messaging of what their product is, what their service is, why it's the best, cheapest, etc. This is basic 101 level marketing. An advanced marketer positions *"how"* they do something. Their messaging includes what their distinction or differentiation is. You many have heard this sometimes referred to as their unique selling proposition or USP. This is what a lot of marketers teach in the marketplace, yours truly included. In an upcoming section of this book I cover in detail how you build your unique USP as part of your marketing tool kit. There's nothing inherently wrong with this, it's just that I believe to truly build an empire and create a tribe of raving fans, there is a whole 'nother level of communicating to your audience that you should embrace as part of your messaging.

Some of the most successful companies in the world today are masters at telling you *"why"* they do the things they do instead of *"what"* they do. Very few businesses or marketers tell you the meaning behind their product, service, objective or mission. Raving fans and customers don't buy what you do…they buy why you do it. Now when you start to communicate from a position of why, all of a sudden your audience starts to listen to you with a different ear so to speak. They tend to emotionally and intellectually connect with you, your brand or your message on a different level because you have now shared with them a sincere, from the heart message instead of just another marketing pitch.

For example, most traditional marketing messages in the marketplace sound like this: We make chef knives (what)…Ours have triple forged titanium steel all the way through the tang (how)…that's how our knives are the lightest and sharpest in the market, wanna buy one? Now compare that message with this one starting with why:

"We believe in thinking different. We build beautifully designed, hand-crafted tools that unleash your creative potential to help you change the world, one meal at a time. Wanna buy one? See the difference? More importantly, did you feel the difference in that last message? This type of messaging has helped create some of the most revered companies and brands on the planet. When you share with people your cause, your purpose, the reason you get out of bed in the morning—it's powerful.

This a Game Changing shift for Rock Star Chefs.

Desire: Ya Gotta Want It!

To achieve any worthwhile goal, vision, or purpose, you must have an overwhelming desire deep in your soul. Napoleon Hill wrote, "*Whatever the mind of man can conceive and believe, it can achieve.*"

An unquenchable desire is the starting point of all accomplishment. Just as a small flame can't heat up a large sauté pan, a weak desire can't produce much in the way of results. Another word to describe an unquenchable desire is "passion." How badly do you want to fulfill your goals and dreams? Is it something that consumes most of your waking thoughts? Do you find it difficult to fall asleep at night, because your mind is racing a mile a minute with ideas and dreams?

Are you willing to do whatever it takes for the chance to live life entirely on your own terms? If so, then every morning, you must wake up jazzed because you are taking action on the thing that means the most to you. Your goal will be to design your life so that you *live to work,* not work to live. We spend so much time at work, why waste that time doing anything other than what we love most? Time is precious, and life is too short to waste a minute of it doing something you don't love, with people you may not even like being around. You owe it to yourself and your family to make massive changes for the better in your life!

In the New Economy and Digital Age, Skills Are Cheap, but Passion Is Priceless!

Unfortunately most people don't have passion and desire in their lives. So they live each day in a sad, numb existence. They are just barely earning a living, eagerly anticipating the week or two of vacation they are "allowed" to take each year. You, on the other hand, will design a life around YOUR schedule. Think about a life in which you take vacations when, where, and for as long as YOU choose.

Don't be one of the herd, just settling for what life has turned into. There is simply no excuse for anyone alive today in the Internet age to suffer through their adult life working at a job they don't love, all in pursuit of a paycheck.

Choose to Achieve More than Ever Before

Purpose, Passion, and Execution (Crawl, Then Walk, Then Run)
In order to achieve any measurable degree of success in your life, you must first define a *purpose* for your achievement: your smokin'-hot reason *why.* You need to know the reasons for why you are doing what you are doing. You need to be very clear on the outcomes that you desire. For example; maybe your "why" is that you currently earn $75,000 per year and in 18 months you want to be earning $150,000 per year so that your spouse can stay home with the kids. That's quite a jump in income, so what will you have to be doing differently in your life to earn that kind of money? What skills or knowledge will you have to gain to earn that kind of money? When you have clearly defined your reasons like this, it kicks your emotions in gear and that helps motivate you.

There is no right or wrong "why." This will be a thought provoking and personal discussion that you must have with yourself so that you get absolute clarity on the outcomes that you desire. Do you want to start a new business because you want to set your own hours, so that you can spend more time with your family and loved ones? Do you want to own and build your own business or product line, so that you can achieve financial security? Or perhaps you want to move into a different neighborhood or bigger house. Unfortunately, most people are not clear on what they want out of life and why they are doing what they are doing day to day. It's one of the reasons that the quote "most men lead lives of quiet desperation" rings true for a large part of our population. Each of us will have our own personal reasons for working hard to achieve the goals that matter to us. So when you develop your statement, keep in mind that we human beings make decisions based on either of two choices: avoiding pain or gaining pleasure.

Why is this important? Because we tend to make decisions primarily to avoid pain. So when you are writing out and phrasing your goal, put it into words that associate *pain* with not staying on task and progressing toward your goals. Think of it as a gift to yourself and your family. Associate more pain with quitting, giving up, and not achieving your goal than you do with completing it. If you don't have the strong purpose, you will quit when things get tough.

Pride of Performance—Pride in Your Work

As you are building your brand for yourself or your business, one way to stand out in the crowd is through excellence. Excellence comes from taking pride in what you are doing, and doing it to your absolute best. And not just on the big things, either. Since most people in our industry are happy with the usual standard of acceptability, whenever someone goes that extra mile or shows enthusiasm in the little things people sit up and notice. Besides, look at how many other restaurants and other chefs there are in the marketplace. How do *you* stand out?

Now, don't confuse pride of performance with ego. Actually, it represents the opposite: *humility.* The quality of the work and the quality of the artisan are inseparable. Halfhearted effort doesn't produce *half* results; it produces *no* worthy results at all. You may have heard the saying "Every job is a self-portrait of the person who does it." Make all your work stand out from the "good enough" efforts of the masses.

Excellence doesn't mean high cost, either. Some of the things you are going to be doing online actually play *better* if they look as though they were done on a budget. The problem with most of corporate America and your competitors is that they equate expense with quality. Nothing could be further from the truth.

Creativity (Yes, It's in You)

To truly stand out in the world and to make a name for yourself or your business, you must have the ability to transcend the same old tired ways of doing things. Create new ideas, concepts, patterns, and services. Rock Star Chefs break the rules all the time (nothing illegal or even remotely unethical, of course) and write completely new rules or change the game completely.

One cautionary note about creativity: all the creative ideas and programs in the world won't mean a thing without execution. Execution is what puts money in the bank, and it's what brings you closer to your dreams and goals. We have a running joke around our offices that goes something like this: "The last friggin' thing we need around here is another *creative idea!*"

Attitude—Yours Will Determine How High or Low You Will Go

One of my favorite authors, Jim Rohn, has an old saying: "Your attitude determines your altitude." I think those few words sum up why so many people are *not* successful. Most quitters blame everything and everyone for why they are not where they want to be in life. The thing they have never quite been able to grasp is this: having a positive attitude will open more doors for you in your life than just about any other single thing.

Jim also stated some of the most profound words of wisdom for Rock Star Chefs: *"Don't wish it were easier; wish you were better."*

Self-Confidence

All Rock Star Chefs believe in themselves and their abilities. Now, please don't confuse self-confidence with ego. You may not know the exact path, but your faith in yourself—your belief that you will make it happen no matter what—is what will carry you across the finish line. Self-confidence also allows you to be flexible and adaptable as things move along toward your dreams and goals. Confidence comes from *competence.* The more you know how to do something, the more comfortable you are doing it. Many of the action items in this book may be new activities or strategies for you. Don't worry, as with everything else you have learned how to do in your professional life, I have full confidence that you will master these new skills just as easily as when you first learned how to filet a fish, make a hollandaise, or bake a perfect soufflé.

Focus

You must either have or develop the ability to narrow your attention and concentrate on the task at hand. As entrepreneurs and creative people, we sometimes fall victim to the "shiny nickel" phenomenon.

Let me explain. One of the members of my Internet marketing mastermind group was taking his turn presenting the status of his online business to our group at our quarterly meetings. All of us in the group were confused about why he was talking about a completely different concept that had nothing to do with his core business.

He was passionately explaining about this new venture and proudly showing us all the Web work that he and his son had done. The major problem, which we all saw immediately, was that this site and service would appeal to about five people in the whole country. Mind you, my dear friend makes MILLIONS in his core business, but he had gotten a little bored and thought this "shiny nickel" would be a cool business to go into.

We immediately helped him see the light and got him back on track before he could get distracted and lose his focus. Needless to say, we probably saved him big bucks and kept him from wasting time on a project that was a no-hoper.

Determination

When you are blazing your own trail you have to have the resolve and sense of purpose to keep you forging ahead regardless of the obstacles and roadblocks that are bound to come your way. Determination will also give you amazing resiliency in recovering from setbacks, adversity, and undesired outcomes.

Rock Star Chefs know that it's not a question of *if* setbacks will come along, but only a matter of *when.* Do all you can to anticipate them and be prepared when they do show up. It's all a part of the process. Remember, if it were easy, everyone would be successful. One of my great Chef mentors once shared this wisdom with me; " *Life is all about how YOU react to the events, both good and not so good, that happen to all of us…you may not be in control of what happens to you, but you are in complete control of how you react."*

Persistence

Persistence goes hand in hand with commitment and determination. You must make a commitment to finish what you start. When you are exhausted, scared, frustrated, and all alone quitting looks good.

Almost every successful Rock Star Chef I have interviewed or worked with counts persistence as the *number one reason* for their success.

"Failure" just wasn't in their vocabulary. Sure there were roadblocks, hits, and misses. But Rock Star Chefs simply endure and press on! Any journey to greatness has its share of setbacks and crap. And by crap I mean criticism, rejection, and a**holes. Look, if success were something you just signed up for, everyone would be doing it. Persistence is self-discipline in action.

> *"Nothing in the world can take the place of persistence. Talent will not; nothing is more common than unsuccessful men with talent. Genius will not; unrewarded genius is almost a proverb. Education will not; the world is full of educated derelicts. Persistence and determination are omnipotent."*
>
> **—Calvin Coolidge**

Hard Work

I save this topic for the end of this chapter. We've covered many of the ingredients for success in the previous pages. Each one of them is a critical part of the journey you are on. But they won't take you all the way to your goal or make your dreams reality without **H-A-R-D W-O-R-K!**

Rock Star Chefs realize that grinding it out day by day is what will get them across the finish line. Excellence is not something that happens by accident or sheer dumb luck. It takes preparation and character. My grandparents called it "work ethic," and my parents and mentors call it "hustle." Everyone likes to win, but how many are truly willing to put in the effort and time to prepare to win?

It takes sacrifice and self-discipline. It is often said that LUCK and OPPORTUNITY often show up disguised as HARD WORK! My good friend and mentor Brendon Burchard put's it this way; *"When You Knock On The Door of Opportunity, Don't Be Surprised That It's WORK That Answers That Door"*

The Work You Do on *You*

Of all the activities you will engage in as you embark on your road to success, the work you do on yourself will be some of the most profitable effort you ever expend. Along this journey, you will need to expand your comfort zone and gain new skills to handle the challenges that invariably come up. As you grow your brand you will need coaches, mentors, and other subject matter experts to help guide you through the minefield.

Don't be stubborn or cheap—these people will save you time, money, and aggravation as you build your business. The skill set you currently have won't solve the challenges you are going to encounter. Invest in yourself; implement what you learn from these experts; and watch your results happen bigger, faster, and more easily.

Cooking Talent

I wanted to save this point for last. It's a given that if you are reading this book, I am going to expect that you have great cooking skills, a developed palate, and the ability produce food that people would be willing to pay money for.

All the tips, techniques, and insider secrets I'm going to share with you won't mean a thing if you can't execute good food consistently and profitably. The proof is in the pudding, so to speak.

Key Ingredients or Principles in Your Recipe for Success

- Map Out three to five major goals for your business and life, and actually put a "by when" date that they will be completed. (For example, "Update the Web site this week," or "Build a social media presence on the major platforms within the next two months.")

- Define Your "WHY," and spell it out in words. What is driving you to jump out of bed in the morning and is engaging all your energy?

- FOCUS! Life is full of tempting distractions. Don't fall victim to them. Keep your eyes on the prize.

- H-A-R-D W-O-R-K! Any worthwhile goal takes time and effort. If you're looking for a quick path to riches, I can't help you, because I don't know one.

- The power of coaches and mentors. Every great achiever has had coaches and mentors along the path to greatness. Don't try to go it alone. Learn from those who have already been there. You don't have to make the same mistakes they did—you should be making *completely new* mistakes.

CHAPTER 2

INTEGRITY

"A cook is creative, marrying ingredients in the way a poet marries words."

—**Roger Verge**

Maintain Your Reputation: You Earned It; Now Keep It Shiny.
The world is effectively shrinking, and the culinary world is even smaller! I am constantly amazed at the number of new people that I meet, only to find that we have a friend or colleague in common. There's a saying in the food business: "everybody knows everybody." Over the course of your career, you will constantly be reminded of this eerie maxim. My point here is that you never want to burn a bridge or be disingenuous with ANYBODY! When you least expect it, it will come back to you and bite you in a painful spot.

It's a lot like how I imagine the Hollywood studio scene to be: life is full of surprises, and the assistant you have today could be your boss tomorrow—better that she or he should like you. At the very least, someone from your past will be an influencer or "gatekeeper" to a decision maker you are trying to woo. Always strive to protect and maintain your name and the quality of your work. I'm not saying that you need to be a brownnose, sucking up to everyone, but you need to be consistent and to be known as a stand-up person. How you treat those who work under you and those who can't immediately benefit you will come back to you in spades—the good as well as the bad.

Now, I know that some situations are unavoidable and even the best-laid plans can fall apart. There are also some people who are just plain dreadful and don't get along with anybody. How you handle yourself, the situation, and others around you will be the factors that most people will remember if something goes down the wrong path.

Your reputation is the public perception of your integrity. Because it's based on other people's opinion of you, it may or may not be accurate. Others may affect your reputation, but only you determine your integrity.

Everything I mentioned above relates to your restaurant's or brand's reputation as well, especially in the digital age! Think about it. Go to your favorite search engine and type in your name or the name of your restaurant. What did you find? What shows up in the search results? Are you even aware of what's being said about you or your joint? Simply put, word of mouth has morphed into *world* of mouth, thanks to the Internet.

Now, lots of people, hearing the words "digital age," immediately assume that it doesn't pertain to them. Make no mistake about it: even if you have never physically touched a computer, your life is being digitally chronicled, ranked, rated, and quantified by others this very second! For example, my daughter posted a video from her smartphone to her Facebook account, showing her grandpa singing "happy birthday" to her from the restaurant where we just celebrated and had dinner. This is a great example of a digital footprint.

The Digital Age has forever changed our lives and our legacy. Most of us don't realize that whether we like it or not, our personal and professional life is available for the whole world to see in an instant.

Each of us has digital footprints all *over* the Internet. These are the relevant content, comments, photos, reviews, social media accounts, and other digital material that we have posted online.

In addition to these footprints or digital artifacts, we also have digital echoes—comments, pictures, or content that others have uploaded about our restaurants or about *us*. (Remember the birthday celebration I mentioned above?) Collectively, these two things have changed the world forever, and as future experts in the New Digital Economy, we'd better get used to this new reality. Besides, websites like Pinterest and Instagram are becoming more popular, with millions of people joining every day. The greater benefit of these "visual inspiration sites" is that they are driving a ton of traffic to brand Web sites that have the smarts to engage with consumers on them. You and your craft are direct beneficiaries of this activity—can you guess why?

Some of the most popular content that is shared on these sites consists of recipes and pictures of food! Facebook thought so much of the potential in this activity that it purchased Instagram for over a billion dollars! Not bad for a company that had been in existence for only a little over a year and had about fourteen employees. Are you seeing the opportunity yet?

Commitment: It's Not a Sprint; It's a Marathon.

Integrity and wisdom are the two pillars from which to build and keep your commitments. You never want to be known as the person who failed to show up for a gig, missed an event, or blew off a customer. No matter how small you may think the gaffe was, someone is going to remember it very differently from you, and they will in turn tell anyone who will listen about how you don't honor your commitments and can't be relied on.

On your way to becoming a Rock Star Chef, you want to stand out from all the people who don't take EVERY ONE their commitments seriously.

Responsibility

Rock Star Chefs who have great character accept responsibilities. They make decisions and determine their own destiny in life. This is a two-edged sword, however. Accepting responsibilities involves taking risks and being held accountable for the outcome. For many people, this is uncomfortable.

Most people would rather stay in their comfort zone and live passive lives, without taking on challenges and responsibilities. They go through life *waiting* for things to happen rather than *making* things happen! Responsible people know that the world owes them nothing.

With the advent of disruptive and easily accessible technology, for the first time in history, each of us has the power to create and leave an influential mark on the world forever—we *all* have the power to become digital celebrities and influencers. The simple fact that what we do today is being recorded for eternity is a radical new concept to most of us, and it can be overwhelming! Where, exactly, does our privacy end and our legacy begin?

You create a legacy of leadership by what you do now. You can choose today to embrace this new digital world and become a leader who empowers others to achieve their best. (We'll discuss the concept of *servant leadership* throughout this book.)

You must completely understand how to navigate going forward in a fully transparent society. Today, anything you say or do online or offline will likely find its way into the digital world. And this becomes truer with every passing day.

No longer do we have the luxury of both a private and a public life—they have become one and the same. In the wake of all the latest Internet scandals by politicians, actors, sports stars, and unknowns, does anyone still believe that anything we do, say, or post online won't be found out?

I remember reading a quote from John D. Rockefeller (an original Rock Star Businessman) that really summarizes this section in this chapter. His quote goes something like this: ***"Next to doing the right thing, the most important thing is to let enough people see you are doing the right thing."***

Integrity: Your Moral Compass

One of my favorite descriptions and examples I give to my daughter about the meaning of integrity is, "Integrity is doing the right thing, at the right time, whether anyone is looking or not." Integrity is that little voice inside you that instinctively knows whether what you are doing is right or wrong according to your own moral compass. The great thing about this concept is that in today's culture, true integrity is more often than not the exception rather than the rule. When you are conducting your life or business in an ethical manner, people will seek you out like a beacon in a storm.

Social Responsibility

Rock Star Chefs have a real chance to affect the world and benefit organizations that serve, at the same time they are building their brand. I talk more about giving of your time, talent, and money in a later chapter, but it's important to change your mind-set a bit right now. Besides, when you start your search to find a great nonprofit organization to work with, you will encounter some amazing individuals who are truly trying to make a difference in this world.

When you hear their stories of why they created the service or organization they did, it will humble you. With the nonprofit I am currently working with, the stories of the people it serves will make all the crazy stuff we do in this business seem insignificant and petty compared to the life-changing actions of the members of this group.

Most people plan to donate to charities and nonprofits *after* they start making some money. Let me shift your thinking a bit. Would it surprise you to know that you can do BOTH at the same time? As a matter of fact, I have seen it happen time and time again—you can actually achieve your personal financial goals FASTER when you are on a parallel path to benefiting others at the same time you benefit yourself and your family.

Online Reputation Management

I think it's good practice in the modern digital age to watch, search, and listen regularly to what is being said about you, your brand, your restaurant, or your products and services. The larger your business is, the more consistently you MUST be paying attention to what is being said about you online. The Fortune 500 companies employ many "listening" platforms that are worth every penny of their monthly five- and six-figure costs. At countless corporate headquarters all over the world, entire teams have as their sole job responsibility to respond to upset customers or negative Internet postings about their company.

To a disgruntled customer in the New Digital Economy, seconds seem like hours, and hours seem like days. The longer it takes a business to respond to a negative comment online about its brand, product, or service, the larger the PR nightmare becomes! This is just a harsh reality of doing business in the online world. Thankfully for the small-business owner or entrepreneur, there are low-cost or no-cost tools that you can use to "listen" to what is being said about you or your business. In just minutes, you can set up a simple Google Alerts campaign for keywords that you choose about you, your business's name, your products' names, and so on.

This will at least give you some basic insight and a starting point from which to monitor your reputation, deserved or not, so that you can maintain your good name or at least respond to damaging comments online. We have created a step-by-step video at

www.RockStarChef.com/googlealerts

Key Ingredients in Your Recipe for Success

- Keep and maintain your reputation. It's a small world now, thanks to social media. Everybody knows somebody who may know everybody.
- Commitments: make them and keep them.
- Integrity: there is only one way to conduct yourself.
- Help make the world a better place.
- Set up alerts to monitor and respond to any posts, articles or links about you and your brand.

CHAPTER 3

SALESMANSHIP: YOUR USP

"A cook, when I dine, seems to me a divine being, who from the depths of his kitchen rules the human race. One considers him as a minister of heaven, because his kitchen is a temple, in which his ovens are the altar."

—**Marc Antoine Desaugiers**

What's the Specialty of the House?

When I consult with my Fortune 500 clients or Celebrity Chefs, one of the first questions I ask the executive or business management team is, "**What makes you, your company, or your products unique and different from everyone else in your competitive marketplace?**" It might surprise you to know that very few could actually articulate in a few simple words or phrases what *truly* made them special.

Oh, they gave very corporate-sounding buzzwords, mission statements, catchphrases, and pitches that sound great at the home office. But out in mainstream America, where most customers are constantly asking themselves, "*What is this?*" and "*Why should I care?*" their words sound like advertising gobbledygook designed to stroke the egos of the marketing alpha dogs that created them.

My task was to politely show them that unless you are Apple or Steve Jobs, the marketplace has a herd mentality and is filled with plenty of "me too" products and services with no real discernible difference between them. Worst of all, most of the items these management and marketing teams offered were never really all that unique or different. They didn't attract a cult following or brand loyalty, and sooner or later, the moment the next "new thing" or new promotion came along from the competition, customers would switch and spend their money with the other guy. As you can imagine, that last statement was not what my clients expected or wanted to hear!

My point is to illustrate that to become a Rock Star Chef, you must separate yourself from the noise of the competition and rise above it by always thinking of your customers and the conversation going on in their head when you are marketing to them. They are asking themselves two fundamental questions: "*What is this?*" and "*Why should I care?*"

I covered the topic of *"why"* you do what you do and how to incorporate that level of messaging into your marketing in an earlier chapter. If you take the time and honestly put yourself, your product, or your services through this scrutiny, you will be light-years ahead of 90 percent of your competition. Here is your new mantra: "***Who am I, what do I offer, why do I do what I do and why should the customers care?***"

It All Starts with One Great Idea

The restaurant and food service industry is rich with examples of how an entrepreneur with one great idea built a great company, introduced an entirely new category to the marketplace, dominated an industry, or even built a whole town around a hot idea. (Ever hear of Hershey, Pennsylvania?)

A hot idea can accomplish all these things. On the other hand, a lukewarm or downright bad idea can dig you deep into a hole before you even get started down the road to profits. I have seen businesses move so far in the wrong direction with a bad idea they thought was hot, by the time they realized the error of their ways it was very costly to get back on track! At the end of the day, it's all about strategy, intelligent positioning, flawless marketing, and disciplined execution. If your brand, product, service, or targeted audience is flawed or off the mark to begin with, there's not a whole lot you can do to achieve success. Want proof? Try selling high-grade, limited-availability grass-fed organic beef to the vegetarians who are in town for the national convention of People for the Ethical Treatment of Animals (PETA)!

So where do all these great ideas come from, then? How can you tell a great idea from a dud idea that has no chance in hell of making it? Well, my friend, that is the question of the day, isn't it? And beyond common sense, there aren't any hard-and-fast rules to help you sort it out. No, Chef, you have to play your hunches—listen to your gut feeling that tells you you're onto something.

Of course, you have to play it smart and have backup information or data that at least can speak to why you *might* be onto something. I can hear your thoughts right now: *All this is easier said than done.* Well, hey, if cranking out a new business idea were easy, then we ALL would be rock stars!

I have people coming up to me all the time sharing with me how frustrated they are that every menu or concept style, every culinary business opportunity, or every idea for a cookbook has been saturated in the marketplace to the point of silliness. The younger generation of chefs and restaurateurs especially are given over to this defeatist (and erroneous) thinking. From their limited perspective, this is how the world appears. They either think that all the good ideas have been taken, or they're intimidated by their lack of knowledge of how to do things. After all, culinary colleges don't really offer a course on how, exactly, to create a new product, idea, or business and successfully take it to the masses in the marketplace.

So what's a budding—or successful—entrepreneurial chef or restaurateur to do? So glad you asked! First thing, quit coming up with lame excuses for why something won't work, can't work, or is already dominated by someone bigger in the marketplace. Want a simple example? Who in the industrialized world hasn't seen or walked by a McDonald's restaurant? No one, that's who. McDonald's is far and away the largest concept in the world that is selling hamburgers… yet who can argue with the continued success of In-and-Out Burger, Five Guys Burgers, Shake Shack and hundreds of others that are quite successful at selling top-notch hamburgers? Heck, these joints are frequented by people who would never even *think* of setting foot inside a Mickey D's!

Each of these smaller companies found its niche or created a different spin against the products served at McD's, and they seem to be competing just fine right there in the giant's shadow. So quit your bitchin' and moanin'! Don't even waste your breath or my time with the excuses—I know them all by heart. Rock Star Chefs realize that great ideas don't fall from the sky into your sauté pan fully cooked. You have to think things through. You have to consider an idea—and then *re*consider every angle on that idea differently from how anyone else in the marketplace has. Study how your potential competitors are approaching their business, and develop better ideas or execution. Think of how you can be unique to your customers and stand out in the marketplace. What is your value proposition? Or, to put it another way, what is your USP?

So What the Heck Is a USP, and How Do You Cook It?

The marketing industry phrase I am talking about is "unique selling proposition," or USP. This simple, straightforward collection of words is what will separate *great* companies from so-so companies. In the A.D.D. world we live in, short, catchy, memorable, descriptive USP's make it easy for current and potential customers to have top-of-mind awareness about *you*. To become a Rock Star Chef, you must brainstorm and create your USP and make it a part of your marketing material and brand identity. It is even more important in the New Digital Economy, where most communication messages are extremely tight (like the 140-character limit on Twitter) due to limitations on the platform or because that's how the audience on those platforms wishes to engage. The days of long-drawn-out marketing messages are over (in print, at least, but we'll cover that later).

Here are some of the most successful and memorable "catchphrases" about a product or service:

- *When it absolutely has to be there overnight* (**FedEx**)
- *Hot, fresh pizza delivered to your door in 30 minutes or less, guaranteed* (**Domino's Pizza**)
- *The thinnest, lightest laptop ever* (**MacBook Pro**)
- *The ultimate driving machine* (**BMW**)
- *Food made with integrity* (**Chipotle**)
- *10,000 songs in your pocket* (**Apple's iPod**)
- *All the world's Web sites in your hands* (**Apple's iPad**)
- *Food as it should be* (**Panera Bread**)
- *Next-level training for the new breed of Rock Star Chefs* (**Rock Star Chef**)

It's Called *What?*

If you can't describe what your product or service is in one or two simple sentences, then you've got the wrong product or service! Seriously, most people are overwhelmed with information overload, and our brains are inherently lazy (efficient). We want to extract meaning and understanding as quickly and effortlessly as possible. If our brain has to spend too much energy in comprehension, it simply moves on. Especially in the age of the Internet and instant everything, our minds want to find relevance quickly. There's an old saying in sales and marketing: *"A confused mind says no."*

Make sure people get what you are all about *quickly.* Don't make your customers or potential customers have to work hard to figure out how to do business with you and give you money. When I was last in Silicon Valley talking with a group of venture capitalists (VCs) about some new projects we were working on, every one of them said that when they are evaluating a company or entrepreneur that is looking for funding, if they can't explain the idea, concept, or business model in a couple of short sentences or paragraphs, they are done! This group will declare the meeting over and get up and walk out of the conference room. How's that for an unambiguous message!

Let me help you out so that the kind of scenario I just described never happens to you or your team. Especially if you ever find yourself in front of a group of potential buyers or investors. Most Rock Star Chefs and culinary professional fall into two buckets. You either have a brand new business idea or you are running a business now and wondering what to do next. Here's the criteria that I use to analyze a business as an investment for either myself or consulting clients when they are looking at an acquisition or investment into a brand or company. By the way, make no mistake that your business or brand is an investment of your time, life energy and money. If it's not serving you and giving you a great return, you need to know it and more importantly, you need to know what to do next.

Here are seven simple questions I ask anyone who has a business idea. These questions aren't complicated and cam be answered in ten minutes or less. These questions can either save you or make you tons of cash if you take them seriously and answer them without any fluff or slick marketing lingo.

1. Is there a market for what you want to sell or provide services for?
2. How large is the market and how responsive is it?
3. Can this particular market be reached, sold to and resold to in a profitable way?
4. Do YOU and your company/brand/service have what it takes to reach it?
5. How can you prove to me or anyone else that #4 is true and realistic?
6. What special skills, talents or proven experiences do you bring to the table?
7. How easy or hard will you be to copy or knock off?

If you get positive answers to these questions, you may very well have something worthwhile to invest in and build. Now, the next step is to test and pay attention to what the market tells you. Don't get emotional or attached to what you want to see happen, let the marketplace tell you what they want to happen by voting with their feet and their wallets. If you don't get clear, positive answers to these questions, it's time to rethink your recipe.

Here's an interesting fact to consider and also show proof that these criteria work: Apple, Google, Facebook and Shake Shack all would have passed this test on their first day as start ups! Apple's original goal was to sell build it yourself computer hobby kits to essentially the same group of guys who also like to do things like get ham radio licenses. Apple was absolutely right about their initial business model projections and hit their target market with the products that their customers wanted to buy. They also had some unique assets (uber tech wizard Steve Wozniak and chief visionary Steve Jobs) that nobody else could copy. Apple would have been a great investment on Day One. The additional 30+ years and hundreds of billions of dollars in profit are simply icing on the cake.

What about Google? Two incredibly smart, hardworking and very meticulous guys had a superior method for handling search on the Internet. Was there a market for Internet search? You bet your ass there was. Since I am from the generation that was the first early adopters of search back in the late 90's and early 2000's, let me share with you the various search engines that we had back in the day. Most of them are gone now, but it's interesting to think of Google being the new kid on the block when it came to search. InfoSeek, Lycos, Excite, Altavista, Inktomi, Ask Jeeves and Yahoo were all making good money from search. Google was a great investment on Day One on that basis alone. The fact that it went on to become one of the biggest companies in the world is a bonus.

What about Facebook? A **proven** model that got college kids to sign up and constantly use a radically new communications platform and digital ecosystem. The unique assets? A maniacally ambitious founder who was able to inspire talented coders into his vision. Was it defendable? Sure was. Once it became the de facto standard for college kids (which it did way before anyone else paid attention), starting and promoting a competing service would have been very expensive and seen as a "me too" copycat. Another great investment from Day One… and the billions of dollars that followed was just a bonus.

Okay, let's get back down to earth and talk about how this relates to all of my culinary brothers and sisters trying to make things happen on planet earth. Apple, Google, and Facebook are all what the investment community calls "moon shots." You can't plan on them and you sure as hell can't predict them. But notice how in each case the original, modest goals of the founders were firmly rooted in reality? I included Shake Shack in my example above to show you that the same business principles that apply to tech start ups also applies to the food service world. As this book goes to print, Shake Shack just completed their IPO and now has a valuation that is in the billions of dollars. The story is almost identical to Apple, Google and Facebook. There was a market. (New Yorkers love great food that is served quickly at a good dollar value) They knew how to reach it in a way that made economic sense. (They opened a fairly inexpensive food cart in a popular park in the heart of NYC) They brought something new and unique to the party. (fresh ingredients, cooked with some culinary expertise at a great price) They had a great chance of defending their position in the market once they created it and now they have to funds to begin their next level of expansion.

Can you answer "yes" to all these things about **your** business idea or the business that you are currently running? This is how investors think and you should start thinking like an investor too about your business and about every business decision you make. It will make all the difference in the world to your outcomes. Guaranteed.

Four-Step Recipe for Product Evolution

Now that you have your USP firmly planted in your mind and you have run your business idea through the seven questions, the next step in your business process is to develop your *go-to-market strategy*. Another term for this is "marketing strategy."

Before we can ever develop a marketing strategy, we have to start out thinking from the product side of the equation. This is the arena where Rock Star Chefs will live, breathe, and die—the kitchen stadium marketplace of ideas! Every entrepreneur must cross these four distinct thresholds on the way to the top. Let me give you an example: Think back to when you first came into a professional kitchen or brigade system. You started off in a very basic role (*Commis*), as either a prep cook or a dishwasher. You then moved up to one of the cold stations (*Garde manger*) where you learned some new skills and, more importantly, how to organize your prep tasks and compose plates that were part of the meal service. Perhaps you then worked the different hot stations on the cooking line: sauté, grill, veg, or expo (cook or *saucier, entremetier, rôtisseur*), and then you moved into one of the managing chef roles. (*sous, chef de cuisine,* or executive chef).

I know that I'm being overly simplistic, but I think you get the general idea that I'm trying to get across: you started out in a basic or limited role and then progressed to an entirely different level. You have gained experience, perspective, and refinement and would now stand out among others just starting out in the kitchen.

Commis → Garde Manger → Station Cook → Chef

Product creation works in much the same way. Referencing the example above, let's hit each stage, one at a time:

When first generating your business or product ideas, start out at the most basic level of the item you are thinking of (*commis*): What is the item or service you are considering? What purpose does it serve? At the most basic level, what type of product, brand, or service are you going to bring to market?

Think of some items that you may see in the grocery store or from your broadline distributor: no-name or generic paper towels or sugar or vegetable oil. These types of items are commodities in the most basic sense—they serve a purpose, but there is nothing fancy about them. Price is often the deciding factor.

One step up from the basic product or service is a recognized label (*garde manger*). This is something that you buy, but you don't really care what it is. Yes, you assume that it is of good quality, but the product is price sensitive. There's a label slapped on there somewhere so that you can figure out who the producer is, but you don't care, because it's not a name you know or will even remember. You are buying this product or service again because of the price and one or two other factors.

On this transaction, you may have bought for convenience, the look, the color, the feel, or simply because it fills a particular need at a particular time. What label can you attach to your product or service?

A brand (cook) is a couple of steps above an item and one step above a label. Now, this is where almost all labels want to be and where most people in the marketplace aspire to be. Usually, the simplest way to accomplish this is with a large bankroll or marketing budget. Brands have an asset or component to them that is immediately recognizable. Maybe it's an identifiable logo, a particular color, or a sound. Price and convenience come into play here as well, but it is also largely about a level of quality, service, or cachet associated with the brand.

A branded product is a known entity, a promise, or a seal of approval. Some examples include Tabasco hot sauces, Driscoll berries, Avocados from Mexico, Old Bay seasoning, Coleman's mustard, etc. What is your brand going to be, and what is it going to stand for? How can a potential customer tell that you are different from your competitors? Why should they do business with you and pay your prices compared to others in the marketplace?

The fourth and final level (executive chef) is a lifestyle or movement. Many of the earlier attributes from the previous categories apply here as well. There is a promise, and there is the same level of trust and value and all those other things I mentioned, but also, this level cuts across a whole line of products or services. It becomes an *integrated product suite*.

And if it is done correctly, there is functional integration that seamlessly weaves itself throughout the entire product suite.

Basic Product → Label → Brand → Lifestyle

A simple example of this is the Hard Rock Corporation. They started out as a restaurant. As they grew they franchised and licensed the name all across the globe. Next, they created clothing and other merchandise that became a *lifestyle* brand. Recent evolution of the company has included retail stores, hotels, and casinos that have branded music clubs within them. There is even talk of creating a time-share resort, an airline, and a branded cruise line similar to what Disney has done.

And speaking of Disney, it is the king of lifestyle or movement brands! Movies, toys, retail stores, destination theme parks, clothing and licensing deals, branded food products, cruise lines, hotels, and resorts—it even has its own island in the Caribbean!

The best example of an integrated product suite in the modern digital age that I can think of is Apple. Think about their entire product suite: iPod, iPhone, iPad, iTunes, iMac, MacBook, Apple TV and now watches. Most of us own at least two or three of these products. We use each of the products seamlessly with the others and by way of iTunes; we have integrated almost all our content across each of the devices. Is there any doubt in your mind that if Apple released any type of new product in the marketplace in the near future, be it a television, a car, a kitchen gadget, a personal assistant robot, or anything else that you would at least check it out and maybe even want to buy it? And you know what? There would be millions of others right behind you, buying anything this company creates. That's powerful, and that is also the type of lifestyle or movement company that Apple has become.

Hard Rock, Disney, and Apple—these are companies and product suites that start out as one thing and grow into a much bigger thing.

And the underlying theme is that there is always the brand name that started it all.

Now, here is the insight and perspective that goes along with the Four-Step Recipe for Product Evolution that I just described. I'll use a couple of old friends and mentors as my example: Emeril Lagasse and Wolfgang Puck. Whether you are a fan or not, these guys are known worldwide by their first name alone and have paved the way with many of the opportunities now available to you and me.

Both these men started out at the most basic level of branding— each was a great cook with humble beginnings. Each began to make a name for himself working at restaurants owned by someone else. They branched out on their own, and each opened up his own namesake restaurants. They further developed these concepts into multiple locations. Of course, cookbooks began to hit the marketplace, and both chefs also created numerous retail product lines that were and are tremendously successful.

There were several spice blends in the marketplace before Emeril made his claim to fame and created his own spice blends, called "Essence." Now cooks at home could create dishes seasoned just like those in Emeril's restaurants. How big and competitive do you think the frozen pizza category was when Wolfgang decided to create his signature pizza line and introduce it to the marketplace? Customers weren't having just any plain old pepperoni pizza for dinner. No, no, now they were having *Wolfgang Puck* pizza for dinner.

Item—Label—Brand—Lifestyle

Both these original Rock Star Chefs launched their own cooking shows on television and even began to produce lifestyle items that were sold on TV or by major retailers. Pots, pans, furniture, flatware, glasses, plates, and spatulas flooded the marketplace.

Now, do you think that if these guys created a hotel, resort, or some other destination venue, there wouldn't be legions of fans eager to spend their vacations and hard-earned dollars there? It seems to have worked for Hard Rock Cafes and Hotels, Chefs Charlie Palmer and Nobu Matsuhara, as well as Dolly Parton and Dollywood! See, I told you there were many similarities between the food business and the music business.

Creating products and services is part art and part science. Throw in a bit of luck and marketplace timing, and you have a winning recipe for success. As you are fleshing out your ideas about what types of products, services, or offerings you're thinking of creating for customers, go back through this section. You never know when an idea will click!

Everything Old Is New Again

One of my online marketing mentors, Ken McCarthy, is an old-school copywriter and direct marketing genius. Ken was one of the first successful online marketers and worked back in the day with Marc Andreessen, founder of Netscape. He has also studied and worked with most of the living legends of the direct-response marketing world: Gary Bencevenga, Gary Halbert, Dan Kennedy, and Drayton Bird. These guys wrote sales and marketing copy back in the day, generating millions of dollars in revenue for their clients and creating fortunes for them in the process. Most of this was pre-Internet—heck, some of it was pre-television!

I mention this because, although the medium may change (radio, TV, print, and now Internet), copywriting is still copywriting, and sales is still sales. It doesn't matter whether it is the written word, the spoken word, or the visual word (think video). The principles are the same, and the ones that worked years ago still work today.

Copywriting is storytelling in print. Even though some of the social media platforms may limit you on the amount of copy you can provide, good storytelling will always intrigue and engage customers. Think of the early days of advertising, depicted in the TV series *Mad Men*. Don Draper and his team not only had to introduce potential customers to products or services; they also had to romance those products with their words. TV advertising was terribly expensive back then, so most brands had to rely on print media or radio. If your ad or promo couldn't convince customers that they just had to have your widget, well, then you just wasted a ton of money and your business was headed for trouble.

There was often long lead-time in magazine ads and direct mail campaigns, so as an advertiser, you had to wait a few weeks before you even could tell if your ad copy worked. Now as direct marketers in the digital age, we can split-test our ads and get feedback in a matter of minutes! We can then adjust a campaign or marketing message accordingly. The old-school copywriters often had to get it right out of the gate or they might never get hired again.

You just need to take the time to learn from these master wordsmiths. Do a Google search on these authors and buy their books. Pay homage to these original rock stars. They have many lessons to teach us!

What Makes You Different from What-His-Name?

To stand out from the crowd, you need to find your "hook"—that special something that makes you rise above the noise that is all anyone hears most of the time. This is how you find your voice or hook for your story:

- Ask yourself, *what would people be shocked to know about me or my specific culinary background, catering services, restaurant, or club?* What would people be surprised to know? There is a big difference between shock and surprise. *Shock* makes people stop in their tracks—and maybe even go away. *Surprise,* on the other hand, stops people for a moment. What would people be pleasantly surprised to know about you or your restaurant? What is it that people always ask but have trouble finding the answer to?

- What have you done? What was your "*aha*" moment? What was the time when you suddenly had absolute clarity and realized why you were doing what you were doing? What is the process you are using, and why is it unique? What is a special recipe, unique ingredient, or drink that you have created, developed, or found? When or what was your breakthrough moment or solution to a problem that nobody else could figure out?

- Clearly define your "story." We all are unique in some way—it is the sum of our experiences that shapes who we are. All stories should be built for a purpose. We all are natural storytellers, and it is hardwired into our brains to respond to stories. It's a way of communicating that most everyone understands. Make sure your story is compelling. What is the one thing you say that really moves people? What is it that, when people find it out, they completely get it and remember you over the competition?

It's All in the Name: Marketing 101

Ever notice how subtle differences in words and descriptions can justify charging more for a menu item at some restaurants or bars? The flowery descriptions or the witty playfulness of the words just seems to jump right off the menu. The words conjure up images in a customer's mind, drawing them in. It's as if a tantric rhythm were moving them without their even being aware of it. Words are things, and the process by which the human mind absorbs those words influences buying decisions.

If you don't think a name makes a huge difference in your success in the marketplace, just ask the producers of prunes in this country. This product suffered a huge image problem due to its name and the images it conjured up. Quick—what image comes to your mind when

I say the words "stewed prunes"? *Yuck …* You probably get an image of old people who are having trouble staying regular. And we've all heard someone described as being "like a dried-up old prune." Not exactly flattering!

So when the marketing association for the prune industry led a campaign not only to change the marketing name but also to also have the federal government change the classification to "dried plums," what do you bet that acceptance and sales of their product grew?

Rock Star Chefs must become terrific marketers, both online and off-line. Let me say that again in a different way: **"Stop thinking only like a chef, and start thinking like a marketer!"** One of the biggest challenges I see with many of my celebrity chef clients is that they don't know how to consistently or strategically market their brands, products, or services. Worse yet, they hire an agent or expensive PR firm that doesn't know how to do it much better.

Look, I'm not down on PR agencies or agents—there are indeed a select few who actually do for their clients the things I am teaching you in this book. I have personally worked with or know many of the top people in London, Chicago, New York, San Francisco, Austin or Los Angeles, and the talent they represent. These individuals are absolute Rock Stars in their field. But when you evaluate the digital marketing campaigns or social media marketing promotions that they create and execute, well, let's just say that the results speak for themselves—and the results are pretty lame!

Hey, I give them credit for at least trying to figure out how to market online. The biggest problem that I see online in marketing for chefs and restaurateurs is that the agencies and agents take exactly the same approach, with exactly same voice, using almost exactly the same words and phrases for *each* of their clients. Yikes!

As you build your brand and start to talk with potential customers, you must also become very good at sales. Salesmanship is tremendously important, but let's not forget that *marketing* allows sales to happen. Before sales (transactions involving customers paying you money) can occur, marketing must be in place to bring the two parties together.

There are a few must-read classic books on advertising and marketing that I have listed in the resource section at the back of this book. You would be wise to buy them and put them to use.

Having the skill set of a great marketer and learning how to do it well is so vitally important to success that I spend over two-thirds of my time at my Rock Star Chef Marketing Academy teaching marketing principles learned over a long career with some of the biggest companies in the world. You can find out more details about the program, as well as when the next event will be hosted, by visiting www. RockStarChefMarketingAcademy.com.

As marketing channels become more and more fragmented, it's going to become even more critical to learn the ins and outs of messaging and positioning for your brand. When you factor in mobile marketing (I define "mobile marketing" as anything related to a smartphone or tablet), the playing field increases exponentially.

To separate yourself from all the "noise" that customers are confronted with daily, you have to design creative, relevant, and engaging content that is a *real solution* for them, not just another marketing pitch or advertisement.

As you've heard me mention earlier in this book, I predict that video is going to be THE preferred modality of communication and messaging on the Web. One very big reason is that video can communicate a burst of information that customers can consume quickly and efficiently, especially on their smartphone as they move about in the world.

This past year, Google indicated that Web use by users of mobile devices is increasing at a faster rate than even Google expected. Since the devices are becoming more powerful, compact, and ubiquitous, broadband is accessible just about anywhere, and we have become a much more mobile society, is it any wonder that mobile devices are preferred over traditional desktop computers?

This is one of the longest chapters in this book, for several reasons. I hope that you grasp how critical it is to shorten your path to becoming a Rock Star Chef by learning how to market yourself, your brand, and your offerings in the most successful ways possible.

Now, for some people, the word "marketing" has a negative connotation. Every one of us understands the image of the cheesy used-car salesman or high-pressure commission-only sales rep who calls you on the phone or sends you spammy e-mail messages trying to persuade you to buy their schlocky product or service. Yes, unfortunately, those people still exist, but thankfully, in the New Digital Economy, their numbers are decreasing. Besides, Rock Star Chefs are servant leaders first, who seek to serve their audiences and customers first instead of just trying to make a quick sale.

Key Ingredients in Your Recipe for Success

- Answer this question: What is so special about you? What makes you unique in the marketplace?
- Define, Develop and Dominate your marketplace with your USP.
- Honestly answer the seven questions about your business or new business idea.
- Develop your product, program, or service and strive to give 5-Star service to your all of your customers and partners.
- Be like Marcus Lemonis, The Profit; business success comes from focusing on People, Process and Profit.

- Become a student of copywriting and study the masters from "back in the day."
- Mobile marketing and video are going to be the dominating channels and platforms in the New Digital Economy. Use this knowledge, and absolutely crush your competition.

CHAPTER 4

EXERCISE AND PHYSIOLOGY

"A crust eaten in peace is better than a banquet partaken in anxiety."

—Aesop

Why Exercise and Physiology?
I'm Here to Become a Rock Star Chef!

One subject you will often hear me discuss in my live workshops or in my training sessions with clients is *presence*. Whether you are in front of customers, friends, or loved ones, creating and maintaining presence during those interactions is the difference between vibrant communication and boring, distracted, hit-or-miss communication. Some people may even describe presence as a person's "energy" or "engagement" level. Now, I'm not talking about someone who's hyper and talking at you a mile a minute. What I am describing is a person we all have encountered at least once in our lives. I'm talking about that person you just remember as making you feel that they were focused solely on you and the conversation you were having with them, in that moment.

Because we as a society are engaging in less face-to-face communication in our lives, it becomes even more important to make the effort to be fully present when you are in front of someone. Just the common courtesy of actually looking someone in the eye when they are speaking to you, and not texting or checking your phone, will go a long way! It has become almost accepted behavior to be multitasking on your smartphone while you are having a conversation with someone. I think this is just plain rude. More importantly, when you *don't* engage in this rude, distracting sort of behavior, people notice, and they truly appreciate your being so present with them. Try it for yourself with the next friend or family member you encounter, and see if you don't agree.

My definition of "presence" and how it relates to physiology is the way you feel, the way you engage, and the way you express with your body. Just about every high-performance achiever I know is a master of this.

Here are several reasons why I believe you must master exercise, physiology, and presence on your road to becoming a Rock Star Chef:

To Feel Good

If you are like most people in modern society, you experience some down days when you are not feeling 100 percent. Your energy level is low, and it seems that you just can't focus. There are several possible reasons for this, but the biggest culprit, overwhelmingly, is *dehydration*. Yes, I know, as simple as it sounds, your body is thirsty!

Unfortunately, most of us try to quench that thirst with every kind of liquid *but* water! Hydration is the key to our bodies' functioning properly and being able to put out energy consistently. Do you know that the cause of most headaches and body aches is dehydration? It's ridiculous when you think of it: it isn't the Advil you take that necessarily makes you feel better; it's the water you wash it down with!

To sustain high levels of energy and presence, every Rock Star Chef needs to stay hydrated and eat properly.

Another key habit of High Performers is that they manage the amount of sleep and rest they get. High achievers make sure to schedule enough time for their sleep and rest periods. Underachievers say they will get as much sleep as they have time for—they'll grab some Z's in whatever time they have left at the end of the day. Perhaps that could be one reason for their low energy and their lackluster performance.

So…are you managing your rest based on your to-do list for the day? It would be hard to accomplish all that Rock Star Chefs want to achieve during their day if they tried to get by on four to six hours of sleep every night.

Managing your food and water intake and your rest will help you achieve all your goals and dreams—and you'll have a lot more fun while you're doing it. This is not just my opinion. There are too many empirical studies on peak-performing athletes and high achievers to dispute this very basic recipe for success.

To Look Good

I'm sure you will agree with me on this: we all want to look good. We all want to be in shape. Regular exercise is the key to a healthy outlook and an attractive body. Internal health is the key to a pleasant external appearance.

Let's face it: if you're going to become a Rock Star Chef, you are going to be onstage in front of people. Whether it's live or via video, ours is a visual medium. You want to be vibrant and full of life. Consistent exercise and a diet of healthy food will help you along. Your health directly influences everything in your life. And I mean *everything*: your wealth, happiness, intelligence, sex life, and longevity.

And that's just the short list! Every aspect of how you live and feel depends on the way you exercise and what you eat. Try to be the best "you" that you can be.

To Reduce the Risk of Heart Disease

Daily exercise helps strengthening the heart muscle. It helps maintain desired cholesterol levels, and it reduces your chances of stroke and the risk of heart disease.

Those of us in working kitchens tend to taste things throughout the day, and not all the things we taste have the healthiest ingredients or the best balance of nutrients. We need to be aware that we put our bodies through different kinds of stresses that most of the population doesn't. I'm simply pointing out that we need to be conscious of everything that passes our lips.

To Lower Blood Pressure and Relieve Stress

As I said, our industry and the nature of our work involve a certain amount of stress. There's no getting around it.

Those of us working in a high-profile kitchen, where every plate going out to the dining room has the potential to make or break reputations, have it even worse. Daily exercise lowers blood pressure and improves circulation. Exercise helps shed and keep off excess body weight and thus helps lower the blood pressure in another way. Exercise burns calories. If supplemented with proper nutrition, exercise will prevent obesity.

To Reduce the Risk of Diabetes

This is one of the scariest rising statistics in our country. Daily exercise helps reduce the percentage of fat in the body, thus reducing the risk of diabetes.

To Reduce the Risk of Osteoporosis

Regular exercise strengthens the body's bones and tissues and helps increase bone density. Thus, exercise serves as an effective means to reduce the risk of osteoporosis.

To Increase Longevity

Daily physical activity is the key to a long life! Regular exercise helps prevent obesity, which is one of the important factors responsible for many life-shortening diseases. Exercise helps reduce the risk of diabetes, cancer, and heart disease.

Research has shown that people engaging in a daily physical activity live longer than those who don't exercise. Remember, Rock Star Chefs want to be around for the long haul. We don't subscribe to the motto famously attributed to James Dean: "Live fast, die young, and leave a good-looking corpse."

To Improve Balance and Reduce the Risk of Injuries

Exercise is found to improve the body's balance and coordination. Because regular exercise strengthens the bones, muscles, and connective tissues of the body, it greatly reduces the risk of severe injury. This keeps us in the game, where we belong, and not recuperating at home in bed.

To Stay Productive

For those of us who have reached certain age milestones in our lives, this next point will ring true. Regular exercise reverses the natural decline in metabolism that sets in after the age of thirty. Those who exercise regularly are found to remain more productive and energetic during the day. A half hour of exercise every morning can help you feel fresh and energized the rest of the day.

To Increase Overall Strength

Exercise is found to increase overall body strength. Rigorous exercise also brings about an increase in physical stamina. And the subject of stamina, for both men and women, is the perfect segue to bring us to my next point….

To Have a Fantastic, World-Rocking, Bone-Rattling Sex Life!

This is my favorite benefit of regular exercise! I don't care if you're single, married, or in a committed relationship—regular, fulfilling sexual activity is a key component of happiness! When you exercise you feel good about yourself and your body, and that's attractive to others, including those whom *you* might find attractive.

The Camera Adds Ten Pounds

I know that diet, exercise, and obesity may be sensitive subjects, but hey, we're all friends here, and it needs to be discussed. Let's face it: our industry is not known for having the healthiest individuals around. All too often, the image of a professional chef is not flattering—a stout, heavyset person usually comes to mind.

Yes, I know that lately we see many new examples of svelte, fit chefs who are preaching a new way to look at food and health. Well, it's about time these folks got the recognition and accolades that they so deserve. The image of the jolly, rotund chef is a caricature that we need to get rid of once and for all. Reality is a cruel mistress sometimes, and you must be aware that as you pursue your Rock Star Chef dreams, looking your best counts, especially in the instant-video age we live in.

Now, I realize that one of the most famous chef quotes is "*Never trust a skinny chef,*" and to some extent I agree. However, for our own health and longevity, we must strive to maintain a proper weight balance. The appearance of normal people and those depicted in high-gloss food fashion magazines may be worlds apart, but more and more Americans are realizing that there can be a balance. A happy medium is possible between being overweight and fashion-model skinny.

Don't Worry, Be Happy

Being active is a great stress reducer. Exercise is believed to generate "happiness molecules" in your body, thus helping you stay happy. More and more studies come out every day reinforcing the finding that when you exercise you manufacture endorphins that contribute to overall positive moods. Higher energy levels resulting from exercise help keep you fresh and happy—a state of being you can't fake for long.

Following a suitable exercise program can add some fun and brightness to your day. I know that our daily lives can get filled up quickly, but you must schedule this important "me" time for yourself. Your doing this simple activity will benefit everyone around you.

Besides, as you are building your brand, that extra spring in your step comes across in your words, personality, and—especially—video segments. You can just *tell* when someone has crazy energy and passion. It comes through that clearly in their voice and actions. Regular exercise will help boost and maintain that passion you're going to need every day that you are on the path to becoming a Rock Star Chef!

Be Expressive in Your Body

This is the secret of all great speakers, all great performers, and all great athletes. They understand that they have to move beyond their normal expressive range when they are performing or engaging an audience. This technique also works when you're in a personal conversation with someone.

People tend sound the way they feel. Have you noticed that the times in your life when you were having a ton of fun, you were louder and more emphatic in your communications? There's a reason for that.

That is our expressive range—the place where our fun, natural, and present state lives!

We have been conditioned, for most of our lives, to be very unexpressive and quiet. But the thing is, we are hardwired to be storytellers. Once upon a time, we communicated and shared our stories by face-to-face communication. We were also expressive with our face and physical body when we talked to each other or shared information with the group. That's also the way we communicated emotion to each other.

Might this have something to do with why we feel somewhat disconnected in this modern age? It's much easier to communicate via e-mail or text, and as a result, we are losing the art of face-to-face conversation. I have a teenage daughter, and this is a constant point of discussion in our household. The subject of looking others directly in the eyes when you are speaking to them has been drilled into my daughter since a very young age. I worry that her generation won't have the same natural tendency in face-to-face communications that previous generations had.

It is only recently in human history that we have had the capability to communicate seamlessly and constantly with our network of friends, all at the touch of a button. The last statistic that I read highlighted the number of times we check our digital devices to be somewhere around *two hundred per day*!

This is another reason why video has been exploding all over the Web and mobile devices. We are genetically programmed to process many visual cues and actions whenever we engage in communications. Have you also noticed that more and more digital or video content is being shared across the various social media platforms? The equipment to create and share this type of content has gotten more sophisticated and powerful, yet the cost has gone down dramatically.

Your 30-Day Recipe for Peak-Performance Physiology, or What to Do Next

Now, I'm not a doctor, nutritionist, or sports physiologist, and any program of this nature needs to get your physician's approval first. I am not giving you professional, medical, or dietary advice. For that, you should seek out the professional opinions of experts in the fields of medicine and exercise physiology whenever possible. I have to stress that what follows is just my opinion based on personal results and results of friends or colleagues. You are free to do as you like. I am here to present things as I see them on the table in front of you. What you do with them is up to you. (Whew, legal disclaimer out of the way!)

All I am asking you to do is commit to trying out this plan that I and many other high achievers use every day, for thirty days, and see if you don't notice a considerable difference in your energy level, happiness level, and overall productivity over the next month. **What have you got to lose? More importantly,** *what have you got to gain?*

Give yourself the gift of this 30-Day Health Challenge, and I think you will be amazed at the results. This is the same intense program I use with my executive coaching clients to quickly increase performance in all areas of their lives. The steps are not complicated or expensive. Most of them will be simple actions that you can do starting today. Yes, some of the food or ingredient suggestions may cost more than their nonorganic counterparts. You're worth it, though…aren't you?

In no particular order, here are some key ingredients to help you along your Rock Star Chef tour:

1. Get plenty of water. It can be tap water or your favorite imported "designer" water. There are even some producers of oxygenated water that you can find online or in large natural-food stores. I don't give specific amounts here, because every body is different. I will tell you, though, that you need to drink more water than

you currently drink. I tend to drink at least one-half to one gallon a day.

2. Get plenty of calories from high-quality ingredients and food sources. Again, the whole discussion of omnivore versus vegetarian versus vegan, organic versus nonorganic, local farmers market versus grocery store, grass-fed versus grain-fed meats, fresh versus canned, carbs versus low carbs, and all the rest invariably comes up in this discussion. Listen, there are TONS of books on these subjects. Find what works best for you. Obviously, if you have any food allergies, avoid those foods! My good friend JJ Virgin has a program that I have personally tried, and it is awesome! Learn more about her and her programs at www.VirginDiet.com. My experience tells me that in this country, we tend to overthink the whole subject of diets and meal planning. The simple answer is, consume high-quality calories and not too many of them.

3. Get plenty of rest! For most of us, seven to eight hours is optimal. And if you sleep with your cell phone in bed with you or on the nightstand close to your head, don't! I am not a conspiracy-theory kind of guy, but common sense dictates that we should probably keep these kinds of devices away from our heads at least for the seven or eight hours we're asleep.

4. If you take a multivitamin, take one that doesn't have any additives, fillers, or other crap in it. Make sure that if there's a coating, it is of a vegetable base. Or, better yet, forget the multi, eat a diet rich in vegetables and whole grains, and remember to take your vitamin D, omega 3, and CoQ10 supplement.

5. Take vitamin D; Suggest a minimum of 1,000 IU for every 25 pounds of body weight. per day in the morning, unless you are outside more than 90 minutes everyday. I take 4,000 in

the morning and 4,000 in the afternoon with a post-workout shake. For those who don't go out in the sun very much or live in a climate where being outside in the warm sun is not an option throughout most of the year, go up to 5,000 IU per day. This is critical because we used to get our vitamin D naturally from the sun, since we were outside more often. Unfortunately for most of us, the only light we get is from being in front of our laptops or, even worse, a TV screen. Vitamin D isn't just the most important supplement, it's probably the most important biohack from the world of anti-aging and human performance. It is also a regulator for our immune and our neuromuscular system. It's also responsible for processing, digesting, and keeping calcium in our bodies, and it's been reported to be a hunger regulator, which can help us control our appetite.

6. Take Omega 3 supplements, usually from fish oil or krill oil. (500 EPA and 800 DHA). Suggest 350 to 1,000 mg per day with meals. This is important for heart and brain function. Most people don't get enough omega 3 fatty acids, because they come only from your diet. Since most folks aren't eating a varied enough diet, they are deficient in this key item. It's important to know that not all fish oil is created equal. Small doses of high-quality fish oil can reduce inflammation, improve brain function and even enhance muscle growth, but poor quality or high doses can cause more problems than they help solve.

7. L-Orninthine and L-Arginine; Suggest taking 500 to 1,000 mg ornithine and 1 to 2 g arginine at bedtime only. These amino acids mildly stimulate the release of human growth hormone (HGH) and the formation of nitric oxide, which increases blood flow, and ornithine helps to eliminate

ammonia from protein digestion. L-ornithine also increase the amount of HGH in the body while building muscle and reducing body fat.

8. Eat your greens! Fresh organic vegetables such as broccoli, kale, and spinach are great. Spinach is packed with nutrients and protein. Broccoli is packed with calcium and many phytonutrients. Try and add these back to at least one or two of your daily meals. There are also some "green drinks" on the market that contain dried powdered versions that make it easier to get these nutrients into your body.

9. Eat more avocados! Especially Avocados from Mexico since they are indigenous to Mexico with its lush tropical climate and nutrient rich volcanic soil. The area of Michoacán is also the ONLY place in the world where the avocado tree naturally blooms year round, thus Avocados from Mexico are the only avocado that is available all seasons and months of the year…24/7/365. Plus I happen to love the taste and crop of avocados during the holiday and early winter months. I think that the oil content is at its highest peak during this bloom. Avocados are a delicious plant source of monounsaturated fat and there isn't a week that goes by without another study touting the health benefits of eating fresh avocados. Check out details over at www.AvocadosFromMexico.com/nutrition-facts

10. Get your exercise. You must get at least three workouts per week, for a minimum of thirty to forty-five minutes each. You may think you don't have time for exercise in your day, but the truth is, you don't have time *not* to exercise. You MUST fit these workouts into your week if you wish to achieve a high level of vibrancy and health in your life.

Key Ingredients in Your Recipe for Success

- Understand the crucial importance of exercise and physiology.
- Be expressive in your body. We were made to move!
- Accept the 30-Day Challenge.
- For more information on products or services mentioned in this chapter, check the resource section.

CHAPTER 5

EFFICIENCY

"A desert without cheese is like a beautiful woman with only one eye."

—Anthelme Brillat Savarin

Work Smarter, Not Just Harder

Many of the tasks or gigs you must accomplish on your way to becoming a Rock Star Chef are easy to do. They may seem tedious at times, though, and you may get frustrated that you don't always see an immediate benefit from doing them. What you have to realize is that building a brand takes effort and time—*lots* of effort and time.

It's never one single thing that pushes you up to the top. It's often many, many things, done over time, that build a base you can launch from. You are going to learn to identify and focus on the right things for your brand and business and not get caught up in busywork. When you do this you will be amazed at how productive you are during the day, and you will start finding slots in your schedule that you can now reclaim for yourself or for other interests that you decide on—you know, like fun time.

Get Your Prep List Done Fast!

As a chef or culinarian, you've had this drilled into you since the day you first walked into a professional kitchen! There isn't any one of us who doesn't continue the mental and physical daily *Mise en Place* list of tasks that need to be done before our shift or day is complete. In business, as in life, people tend to concentrate on busywork instead of actually achieving results, creating products, or completing tasks. When I consulted with many of my Fortune 500 clients, I would see this happen all too often, and almost every client had the same challenge.

The solution that I offered them—and one that I use regularly in my daily routine—is the Mise en Place Worksheet found in the resource section.

As you can see from the example on the next page, you strive to keep no more than three to five major tasks on your list each day that need your action.

Take Back Control of Your Daily Schedule!

We have a running joke around the office that some of our bigger clients tend to have meetings about having meetings to discuss the idea of… having a meeting! The drill goes something like this:

> First, schedule a meeting to discuss the parameters of the meeting and who should be in attendance at said meeting, as it may pertain to their subject-matter expertise and contribution to the meeting/project goals and deliverables. Once the deliverables have been established, another meeting should be conducted to quantify the measurement of the deliverables and in what

MISE EN PLACE LIST

MAJOR GIGS

Gig #1	Gig #2	Gig #3
5 big things I must do to move this project forward:	5 big things I must do to move this project forward:	5 big things I must do to move this project forward:
1 _____	1 _____	1 _____
2 _____	2 _____	2 _____
3 _____	3 _____	3 _____
4 _____	4 _____	4 _____
5 _____	5 _____	5 _____

PEOPLE

People I need to reach out to today
List the people you have to reach out to today no matter what:

_____
_____
_____
_____
_____

People I'm waiting on:
List the people you need something from to move forward:

_____
_____
_____
_____
_____

PRIORITIES

The main gigs and tasks **I must complete today**, no matter what!

_____
_____
_____
_____
_____

ROCKSTARCHEF.COM

format they should be distributed among the group. Then and only then can a proper and efficient meeting be scheduled.

Whew! I have a headache just thinking about that one.

Now, don't get me wrong, when any company is creating a major strategic initiative or concept, a high-level planning meeting like the one described above is absolutely crucial. But get this: the example I gave above is an extract from an *actual client's memo*. It was sent out in an effort to decide whether to let employees wear casual clothing at the corporate offices on Fridays during the hot summer months! (And JP, if you are reading this, you know who you are.)

One of the best examples of good, efficient meeting orchestration I have ever seen was when I worked with Wal-Mart and Sam's Club. At the corporate offices in Bentonville, Arkansas, there was a strict rule that no meeting would last more than one hour—not one minute more. As a matter of fact, in some of the vendor meetings, you were kicked out of the meeting room by the next group of folks using the space. More things were accomplished in those sixty minutes than most companies get done in week. It seems to work for Wal-Mart, and you can't argue with their success.

"Get your prep list done fast" means not procrastinating, creating to-do lists, or rearranging your desktop, but actually *getting stuff done and completed*. Rock Star Chefs need to move just as they do in the kitchen: quickly, efficiently, and with purpose.

In the online world, sometimes "good enough" is good enough. Allow me to explain. Many of the tasks needed to build your brand and create a buzz about it are going to involve you creating content for the Web. I am not talking about Emmy Awardwinning video or Pulitzer Prizewinning journalism. What I am talking about is creating relevant, meaningful, insightful, and authentic pieces of marketing material. Articles, videos, blog posts, press releases, joint ventures, sponsorships, interviews, and such are what are going to build and promote your brand.

You do not need to spend time and effort trying to create slick, overproduced content. A simple iPhone video or a witty post on your social media sites will do more for you than any expensive, time-consuming marketing fluff piece! You need to have consistent Web presence about you and your brand, and it has never been easier or more cost effective to market like crazy. Remember, **don't just think like a Chef;** *Start Thinking Like a Marketer.*

The 80/20 Rule Exposed

If you Google "80/20 rule" or "Pareto principle," you'll find a ton of information on this amazing and bizarre principle. You have probably heard some form or version of the concept. Basically, in just about any topic, service, or data you wish to compile and study, a ratio of about 80/20 will always organize itself. Yes, there are occasions where the percentages don't measure out precisely to 80 and 20. Sometimes it will be 76/24, or 83/17, but in general and over time, 80/20 wins out.

To most people (if they know what it is at all), the 80/20 rule is not much more than a business buzzword and maybe a handy rule of thumb for setting priorities. But those who truly understand the 80/20 rule's depth and *live* by it possess a secret weapon of immense power. Eighty/Twenty is not just a business rule of thumb. It's a law of nature. When you understand it the way I do, you have the power to completely transform your business and your personal effectiveness at every level. You will multiply the value of your time, free up important resources, and make more money than you ever have before.

I know—I've experienced it myself. The 80/20 rule empowers every business decision I make, and more importantly, I keep making totally new discoveries about 80/20 that make it even more powerful.

What I am about to share with you is the beginning of your journey to getting more done with less effort than you ever knew possible. Once you find out how to identify and measure the tasks that bring you the most results for your business, your life will never be the same.

For example; for a chef, restaurateur or business owner, roughly....

- 80 percent of sales come from 20 percent of your customers,
- 80 percent of net profits come from 20 percent of your menu items,
- 80 percent of the problems come from 20 percent of the customers or employees,
- 80 percent of your payroll dollars are driven by 20 percent of the staff,
- 80 percent of your productivity occurs during 20 percent of your time,
- 20 percent of your customers at any level have the potential to spend four times as much money as they are right now and 4 percent will spend *up to sixteen times more!* (reread this last bullet point a couple of more times)

And so on, but the real gains come from (a) cascading multiple 80/20 relationships together, and (b) applying the successive gains to strategic multistep marketing. It will literally make marketing generate four to sixteen, to sixty-four times the results.

Let me show you the cascading effect of what the 80/20 rule really is—and, more importantly, what it *can* be. In this example, I'm going to use a product or service-based business. That business could be a small winery, a broad-line distributor, or a bakery commissary that supplies various businesses and accounts around the area. This example would also apply equally well to the front-of-the-house staff of a restaurant. Let's say you go out and hire ten new salespeople for your business.

The 80/20 rule says that two of them will produce 80 percent of the sales, and the other eight will produce 20 percent of the sales. Which means, if they're on a commission-based compensation plan (which, in all likelihood, they would be), the guys and girls who are successful make SIXTEEN TIMES as much money as the rest.

That's right, 16X. A sales manager who invests time developing the two top performers gets sixteen times the payoff working with them, compared to working with the worst performers. This proportion is true of customers, employees, managers, departments—you name it. In almost any business, if you look, you'll find literally *dozens* of 16X spreads between seemingly equal people, products, and services. Eighty/ twenty thinking happens when you discover how to identify the number of business elements, products, and market segments that have 16X leverage. Those SIXTEENS start adding up fast. When you have this kind of profit, you push through your current revenue limits quickly.

$$16 + 16 = 32$$
$$16 + 16 + 16 = 48$$
$$16 + 16 + 16 + 16 = 64$$

Simple enough, right? When those 16s start happening, you'll feel like Atlas would feel if someone lifted the world off his shoulders. Sixteen is better than one any day. But here's the thing: you can understand everything I just said and still be leaving two-thirds or three-fourths or even 97 percent of the money on the table. Because adding 16s together is only the tip of the iceberg. The real power is not in *adding* the 16s together; it's when you start *multiplying* them.

$$16 \times 16 = 256$$
$$16 \times 16 \times 16 = 4{,}096$$
$$16 \times 16 \times 16 \times 16 = 65{,}536$$

My fellow chefs and restaurateurs are always amazed when I show them the power of this principle. The real multiplying power of this eludes everyone else's grasp. The number of people I know who truly GET this, I can count on one had. They are even more surprised when they actually implement it in their own businesses and see the results! At my Rock Star Chef Marketing Academy workshops, we cover real-world examples and case studies extensively.

The way that Rock Star Chefs can use this principle to their advantage is by thinking and planning out their daily and weekly tasks around finding and completing the 20 percent of tasks that give them 80 percent of their results. This subject could fill not only an entire chapter, but an entire book. Matter of fact, one of the best on the subject is from Perry Marshall and it's called ***80/20 Sales and Marketing—The Definitive Guide to Working Less and Making More***. I highly suggest you pick up a copy and study this topic in great detail. Perry is a master of this subject and he has extensive training materials, apps and programs available for free at www.perrymarshall.com

Did you notice that this chapter on efficiency was very concise, short and to the point? Hmmmm….

Key Ingredients in Your Recipe for Success

- Work smarter, NOT harder.
- Get back control of your daily schedule.
- Understand and implement the 80/20 Rule for business and your personal life. It's a powerful principle that cannot be ignored.

CHAPTER 6

NETWORKING OFF-LINE

"A fruit is a vegetable with looks and money. Plus, if you let fruit rot, it turns into wine, something Brussels sprouts never do."
—P.J. O'Rourke

I've Never Met a Stranger

As much as I am in awe of the Internet and the profound effects it has had on our world, I worry that somehow our personal face-to-face interactions will suffer if we become too dependent on the Net and on communicating through computer and smartphone screens. Interpersonal skills are vitally important to becoming a Rock Star Chef. Speaking clearly, looking people in the eyes when talking to them, and listening attentively were all things that my parents drilled into me from an early age. I was lucky.

My fear is that we will become lazy and forget some of those basic human interaction skills because we are so used to typing, texting, or voice mailing with almost everyone we communicate with. I mentioned before that I see some of this in my young daughter. She and her friends don't talk on the phone for hours, as teenage girls did when I was her age. They text, IM, and comment on their friends' social media sites. I can count on one hand the times my daughter actually *talks* to her friends on the phone every week.

It's almost scary how fast some of these girls can type with their thumbs! And let's not forget all the word abbreviations these kids text with that would make our grade school English teachers cringe: *"R U feeling wat im sayng?" "LOL," "IDK,"* and *"LMFAO."*

But what passes for acceptable communications between teens is hardly a standard for serious businesspeople. In the real world, Rock Star Chefs go out of their way to meet new people and make them feel comfortable by being cordial, polite, and genuinely interested in the other person's thoughts and opinions. They introduce newcomers to a group and use the other person's first name often during conversation. They also speak clearly, look folks in the eyes, and listen twice as much as they talk. These are individuals who show respect to all. They have manners, they are graceful, and people at all levels of "importance" enjoy being around them.

There! Mom would be happy that her lessons and constant harping on me to show respect and good manners actually took root.

It's Not Who You Know; It's Who Knows *You*

As you are getting the word out about yourself and your brand and meeting new friends, one thought needs to be "top of mind." People must not only know you by name; they should also instantly connect you and your name with what you do. It may surprise you to know that people will associate you with what you do. Women are amazing with this. When I am dating a new love interest, her friends don't always talk about me by my name; they ask her how things are going with "that cute chef guy." Now, "cute" is surely in the eye of the beholder, but the point is, they know I'm a *chef*.

Same goes for you. People may not always remember your full name, but they'll remember what you do or what business you are in. Are you Alexis the vegetarian caterer, or Mike the exotic-game chef? What about Bubba the barbecue pit boss? This is a key to networking. I'm sure you have heard about the "six degrees of separation" phenomenon. Every person you wish to meet, or organization you want to contact, is available to you through no more than six degrees of separation. Somewhere in your circle of friends, customers, and family (a larger circle than you probably suppose, by the way) is a person who knows someone who has a contact who can help propel your efforts.

As you are networking in the real world make sure that you create a positive image and impression of yourself, your brand, and how you can help someone else achieve what *they* want. Don't be one of those people who look at others only for how they can benefit number one. Look at finding out ways that you can serve others and fulfill their needs.

Creating Digital Relationships

Friends and colleagues are constantly asking me how I have created so many relationships online in such a short time. They want to know how I have created massive followings for the brands and product lines I've worked with. My very simple answers to them—and for you to learn from—come down to three basic frameworks:

Show that you genuinely care. Most people who engage in the various social media channels don't follow just the most popular people or the coolest brands. (Think Lady Gaga and Apple.) They also follow and engage at a higher level with people and brands that they truly believe care about *them*.

Think about it for a second. If an actor or musician has fifteen million followers, do you think they personally know each individual they are connected to online? The answer, of course, is no, not a chance. However, the best practitioners of Web 3.0 understand that they need to consistently acknowledge their followers and make them feel important. Thus, they're happy to admit, loudly enough for the world to hear, that their fans are the main contributors to their success. (Again, think Lady Gaga and Apple.) If these huge mega brands understand the power of caring about their online relationships, shouldn't you?

Add value. Provide your audience with real value or solutions. I tell my corporate teams, "Stop acting like a *brand* and start being a *solution* for your customers." Help your customers accomplish what they are trying to do. Make them feel important, and *help them out*. In the New Digital Economy, you give first; *then* you receive.

Be transparent, honest, and disciplined: Be who you are. The world needs more authentic leaders—not just *personas*. I believe that at our core, those of us who have chosen this life are artists in the full meaning of the word. We have doubts, worries, concerns, passions, dreams, and faults. By showing this authentic self, we make customers and fans feel as though we are really letting them into our world and becoming a trusted friend.

If nothing else, it only adds to the relationship, for they see that in many ways, we are just like them. So quit trying to be so perfect or pretend everything is just rosy all the time. There are no successful spin-doctors in the Internet age—at least, not for long. If there were, we wouldn't keep seeing disgraced politicians, actors, musicians, and sports heroes screwing up and being caught out pretending to be something they weren't.

Never Underestimate the Gatekeeper

When you are networking with people, small and large companies, and the media, please, please, *please* treat everyone in those organizations with respect and kindness. And yes, I mean EVERYONE.

I can't tell you how many stories I have heard about a celebrity chef client who has gained a reputation for being a complete ass to the rank and file of an organization, but being all sweetness and light to the boss or someone higher up in the organization who can help them.

Many a career or opportunity has been damaged by someone being brusque or dismissive to an administrative assistant, coordinator, or significant other of someone they were trying to do business with. It goes without saying that you should be respectful and polite to *everyone* you meet, but especially if you're trying to gain access to a thought leader or person who can influence your career and goals.

People talk about the interactions (good or bad) that someone new to a company or program brings with them. I'm not suggesting that you should let people walk over you, but you should always be mindful of how you're coming across to those who work in the organization you are beginning to work with or trying to work with.

Be known as the person who is always polite, upbeat, and respectful and remembers the gatekeeper's first name. Trust me, these people can influence their bosses' opinion of you with a sentence or even a *look* when your name comes up.

Pay for Access

I learned this next idea from a fellow member of my digital marketing mastermind group. At one of our sessions, he shared with me the method of how he goes about meeting a celebrity, business pioneer, or person of influence he wishes to work with. When trying to get an introduction or make contact with someone for a project he is working on, he finds out how he can "buy" his way into that person's world.

Now, since plenty of buttheads have turned people off by trying to take advantage of the situation, "buy" sometimes has a cheesy connotation. So let me explain what I mean. Often, these powerful people may have a training seminar or program, or perhaps they are speaking at an event or fund-raiser. Many of the movers and shakers who can help you have charities or organizations that they are passionate about. When you invest in and support these things that others are doing, you instantly lift yourself up from the masses that simply want something.

For example, let's say there's a thought leader you admire and would like to work with. Say she is conducting a two-day training seminar that costs five thousand dollars to attend. Now, you may or may not want to attend for the actual information she will convey, but consider this: you will have access to that person on the breaks and at mealtime, when you can introduction yourself and build a connection. Who wouldn't be flattered if you came up to them and said, "Hello, my name is…and I just wanted you to know that I flew all the way here to attend your training so that I could meet you"?

Or how about attending a fund-raiser for the person you wish to work with, and becoming one of the big donors of money or services for their event? Don't you think they would at least have a brief conversation with you or take your call the next day when you phone them at their office (and are nice to their assistant)?

Or say you bid on and win a once-in-a-lifetime-experience package at a charity event. Let's say Michael Jordan has donated a package deal to the charity for someone to play a round of golf with him. Don't you think you could possibly have a nonself-serving conversation and mention to MJ what you do or are trying to do in your business or brand? Are you getting any ideas from this chapter?

Many of my Rock Star Chef friends and one of my important mentors have done every one of these things listed above and many, many more.

One underlying thought, however, that they ALWAYS keep in mind when they approach these individuals is….

How Can I Serve?

One thought, one thing, that you must always, always, *always* have in your heart when you are dealing with people is how you can serve their needs, wants, and desires first, before you EVER talk about how they can serve yours. Lip service is not enough—you must be genuinely interested in helping them achieve their goals.

I have four questions that my mentor taught me long ago, which will pretty much blow away any new person that you meet. Why? Because rarely does anyone ever put this sort of personal, thought-provoking question to a professional or personal contact.

The key to the questions below is that they are meant to be brought up in casual conversation—*no*t used like the interrogation sequence from a bad cop movie. Be fun and genuinely interested in the answers you receive. You will notice people come alive and even do a double take because someone actually took the time to discover things that are important *to them*.

1. Is there an organization or project that you are currently involved with that is a source of passion and inspiration for you?
2. What would it take to double your income or revenue in the next twelve months?
3. What would it take to double your happiness or personal satisfaction in the next twelve months?
4. What have you tried in the past to achieve these goals?

Can you tell by the tone of these questions that when you engage someone with this kind of dialogue you become a "go-*giver*," not just a "go-getter"? You are genuinely showing them that you are trying to be a solution, not just a brand or chef pushing a message.

Far too many people, businesses, and even family members come across as self-serving and shallow simply because they have a vibe about them that screams, "What can you do for *me?*"

As you are building your Rock Star Chef brand and networking with the world around you let others know that you genuinely care about them and *their* needs first, over your own. Besides, the law of reciprocity is that we like doing things for others who have done something for us.

Now, there's a fine line between "Hey, I did this for you; you should do that for me" and "How can I serve you, your needs, or your customers?" In the first example, you have become a *creditor,* not a servant. When you come across as genuine, people respond. There isn't much more I can say to explain it in words, but humans can generally tell when you are sincere and when you are full of crap and in it only for yourself.

Key Ingredients in Your Recipe for Success

- Always remember, it's not who you know; it's who knows *you.*
- Create, foster, and maintain your digital relationships.
- Pay for access—it's money well spent.
- Be a potential solution for people.
- Seek first to be of service to others, in this day and age everyone else seems to be looking for what someone can do for them.

CHAPTER 7

PROMOTE, PROMOTE, PROMOTE (AND PROMOTE)

"A good apprentice cook must be polite with the dishwasher as with the chef."

—**Fernand Point**

Welcome to Web 3.0

The quantum leap in income and profit happens when you change from a doer of your thing to a marketer of your thing.

In this next chapter, I'll explain how to use the Internet and many of the social media networking tools and digital platforms to take you from ground zero to building not only a business but a powerful Rock Star Chef brand that makes you money and, more importantly, brings to your work/business life a passion that will create all the happiness and success you can imagine.

I will talk about personal or brand websites, blogs, product websites, social media campaigns, articles, digital platforms, and many other facets of the Web. Don't worry or get overwhelmed. Most of the things I'm going to talk about are simple to execute, and the process of creating and maintaining them is simple. The process will take time, effort, and laser focus, but not a ton of money. This is the game changer I have been talking about. The Internet has leveled the playing field so that EVERYONE has a shot, not only those with deep pockets.

Why do I talk about digital, social, and mobile media so much? Easy: because these three platforms have created an unprecedented venue for chefs, entrepreneurs, and corporations to have dialogue and engage with their customers at unbelievable speeds and with relevant, influential reach. While these tools alone will not *create* your success, they will definitely accelerate it.

What I love about social media and digital marketing is the fact that when you spend money or focus your efforts on these two things, you're not actually investing time and money in a platform—you're investing in a culture and in customers who will ultimately become your greatest fans and brand ambassadors.

I explained earlier how revolutionary I believe the Internet is and how profound an impact it has had on us all from a cultural-shift point of view. I also mentioned how, from a business perspective, the biggest shift is yet to come. It's a little bit scary to think that the commercial Internet is really only about 16 years old! I have been on the Web since the early days of 1995, when dial-up was the only way we could access the Net, and we were happy to do it.

The Internet has matured from an electronic bulletin board system for computer and university geeks into a second home for almost every American—and the rest of the world is fast coming on board and online. What started out as a way for people to stay in contact with friends, family, and colleagues (e-mail) has evolved into a medium where people spend hours researching information, shopping for goods and services, being entertained, and, increasingly, moving their social and professional circles online to sites such as Google+, Facebook, Tumblr, LinkedIn, Twitter, YouTube, Pinterest, Instagram, Foursquare, and Viddler.

I mentioned it briefly before, but did you know that by the time you finish reading this book, mobile will have surpassed desktop as the preferred method of engaging on the Web? Read that sentence again: people now search and spend time on Web sites accessing the content from their mobile toys instead of from their home computers or laptops. What's even more staggering, if you think about it for a moment, is that growing numbers of people actually use their mobile devices EVEN WHEN THEY ARE IN THE HOUSE!

Think about all the iPads, smartphones, Kindles, and other mobile devices that are just as powerful as any desktop and a hell of a lot more portable! Retailers, restaurateurs, marketers, and brand companies are all scrambling to figure out how to serve this audience as habits shift from a single point of access to multiple points of access, to digital content for consumers.

Follow the eyeballs, and you follow the money. As more and more of us spend a larger part of our daily activities online, it only makes sense that this is where money *has* to flow. Advertisers follow audiences.

A fundamental shift has taken place in this new medium. Advertisers used to spend money on the old-guard media outlets: radio, television, newspapers, magazines, and billboards.

Each of these platforms is losing viewers/listeners/MONEY to the online world by the second! What's worse is that many of them reacted too slowly to the threat from the Internet. Take a look at any news article over the past five years and you will see a story of an old-guard newspaper going out of business after being around for decades—some of them for a century or more!

How many magazines have folded due to lack of readership? And how much smaller is traditional radio's audience becoming each year due to increased competition from satellite radio, podcasts, and the Internet. And don't get me started on the plight of television and cable. Increased competition from YouTube, Apple TV, Netflix, Xbox, Hulu, Ustream, and others is a sure sign of things to come.

Every business, from the corner mom-and-pop to the Fortune 500, is experiencing the same thing: marketing has become really hard in this New Digital Economy. As eyeballs shift to new venues, many markets are splintering, attention spans are shrinking, and the amount of information that people are trying to consume and absorb continues to multiply every day.

The Internet is changing whole industries seemingly overnight. Think about the traditional landline telephone many of us used to have in our homes and small offices. I say "used to have" because everyone I know has canceled their service, because…well, remind me, why do we need it anymore?

With the flood of smartphones and voice-over-Internet (VoIP) services such as Skype and Magic Jack, why would you pay so much for something that is now irrelevant? I fear that if traditional television and cable don't respond to the competition and changing consumer habits, they, too, will have to join the other dinosaurs in the museum of extinct business models.

What does all this mean for a Rock Star Chef? Plenty! Think about what I've been describing here. Media platforms are changing radically. Advertisers are looking for nontraditional platforms that their audiences and customers are going to, and these advertisers *must spend money to stay competitive.*

So…don't you want them spending it with you? By building your Rock Star Chef brand using the Internet and social media networks, you are becoming a viable outlet for them to advertise on.

Digital platforms and the mobile Web are the next growth phase opportunity for Rock Star Chefs. Stay tuned; it's going to be fun!

Building Your Brand

We live in interesting times. I don't know about you, but I am constantly amazed by the evolution of technology and the speed at which it is affecting each of our lives in so many profound ways. It is also affecting us in many ways that, some would argue, aren't so great for us as individuals. Think about the privacy issues online, or how we're always "plugged in" to our digital gadgets at the expense of face-to-face interaction with each other. As we build our businesses or brands just pause for a moment and think about how the relationship between customers and businesses has been transformed over the past very few years.

Standing where we are today, it's hard to recognize where we were not too long ago! To be perfectly blunt and honest about it, I wouldn't have been able to achieve the business success I've recently had in my life if not for the technology, tools, and platforms that are available to all of us today. The digital marketplace has forced traditional marketing and advertising agencies to do a complete 180, and a lot of them spun right out—it was just too much for them. The way things used to be in the Old Economy was that tastemakers and brand builders on Madison Avenue or out in Hollywood called all the shots. They told us what was cool, what we should wear, what we should drink or eat, what we should drive, and even how we should furnish our home. It was pretty much a one-way street... until now.

There has been a slight change to the program. Now customers are dictating what *they* want, when they want it, and companies are responding. That's how close the connection has become between businesses and consumers: close enough to generate a very intimate back-and-forth engagement. Customers are now in driver's seat, and that isn't going to change anytime soon.

Your customer in the New Digital Economy desires more and more to engage with you, your brand, product, or service—but on *their* terms. Almost every large marketing demographic (think Baby Boomers, Gen X'ers, Millennials, for instance) will support those businesses and entrepreneurs that they feel they have a connection with. Not just a transactional relationship, but one in which they feel they are part of a movement, an ideal, a community, something else that's special.

My point is that as you build or enhance your brand in the coming years, realize that the customer is going to be engaged much more than ever before in history, and the winners of this relationship will be the entrepreneurs and businesses that embrace this new dynamic of doing business. Don't be just a one-shot type of business, where you do everything in your power to get a customer. Be the type of Rock Star Chef or business who does everything in their power to *keep* a customer.

Who needs one-shot business transactions when there's long-term money to be had? The concept is to build a viable, sustainable, long-term business that serves its audience well. How many one-hit wonders have we all encountered in the music business or the restaurant industry? Too many, if you ask me. Besides, I believe that today's consumer is looking for companies and individuals who conduct themselves for the long haul. Remember, it costs ten times more to market to new customers than to engage directly with current and existing customers. Yes, that's right: *ten times*. And with today's technology, it's even easier and more efficient to accomplish this in record time at a very low cost.

I won't sugarcoat it for you. It also takes ten times more imagination and follow-through to develop and maintain a customer-loyalty strategy instead of a traditional customer-retention strategy. If you really want to stand out from your competition, you must add value to the equation, and you must do it consistently, deliberately, and genuinely. Hey, if it were easy, everyone would be doing it! That's why you are on the path to becoming a Rock Star Chef: you are willing to do that little bit extra for your customers and fans, and they will reward you handsomely for it.

Building Your Brand Online

If you are one of my celebrity chef readers who already have some sort of online presence, I applaud you. You have at least taken action and tried to engage with your audience in the digital space. However, it is not enough just to "have an online presence." I have been to most of your Web sites and social media channels, and I can tell you right off the bat two things that are fundamentally missing from them. Also, by not having them executed correctly, you are leaving BIG money on the table. The good news is, there's a very simple and low-cost way to fix this problem in thirty minutes or less. Are you just a little bit curious to know what those two things are that *everybody* is missing? Here they are:

1. You're not capturing names and e-mail addresses.
2. If you are capturing this information, you're not communicating and adding value to your audience consistently or strategically. Typically, you are either sending them nothing after they sign up, or sending them only marketing messages. Either way, the people who have raised their hand and told you they wish to hear from you are not having that wish fulfilled correctly!

If you are wondering why I suggest that you do this simple yet fundamental marketing technique, let me explain. I was recently working with one of my celebrity chef clients whom you see on TV quite a bit. This chef was releasing a new book and doing all the traditional book marketing tactics: radio interviews, morning TV spots, daytime shows, and so on. Now, this chef has a talent agent, a major New York publishing house, and a high-profile presence on a certain television network centered on food, but NONE of these "experts" suggested that this chef implement what I am about to share with you here.

When I asked my new chef friend (we'll call him or her "Pat") how many books they were going to sell, Pat told me they were reasonably confident they would sell more than a hundred thousand books. I said, "That's *fantastic*! What are you going to do with all the names and e-mail addresses that you collect from people who buy your book?"

This chef looked at me quizzically and said, "Come again? How the heck would I even *know* who bought my book, let alone get their names and e-mail addresses? What would I *do* with that kind of information, anyway?"

With a huge grin, I replied, "Welcome To Web 3.0!"

To explain the concept, I shared this example: Almost every restaurant keeps a mailing list or contact list of its regulars or VIPs who come in. They send out information or other marketing messages about upcoming event nights or special menus that the chef has come up with. The smart marketers will send out birthday or anniversary wishes to this list, as well as any news about upcoming new restaurant openings or cooking classes. Now, this is a very basic approach to marketing, and it really centers on the business's "pushing" out a marketing message. It doesn't really add any value or uniqueness to the relationship between the customer and the restaurant, but it is at least an attempt to engage. Businesses have always known that if they keep a list of their best customers and occasionally market to this list, it can be a significant revenue generator.

Back to the book example. I told my client, "Imagine if you had a list of 100,000 customers across the country (world?) who think highly enough of you to spend their hard-earned dollars—or euros, or pounds, or yen—on something they will keep in their home or give as a present to someone else, who will then keep it in their home or office. These individuals will see your name or the name of your restaurant on a table, in the kitchen, or on a bookshelf countless times. So…isn't your book a marketing message about you or your brand? If you aren't thinking of it this way, you should be!

I explained to my client that in the New Digital Economy there are several ways to get customers who purchased the book to freely and openly give up their basic contact info and possibly even share their mailing address. One simple way to capture this info is to add an **opt-in** request box directly on an existing Web site, or create a simple one-page Web site that has the same address (or URL) as the name of the book.

You can use free or low-cost software (Optimize Press) to create the opt-in box on your Web site, or you can create a one-page WordPress site yourself in just a few minutes.

One way to let customers know about these opt-in boxes and special landing pages is to create a short paragraph, directly on a page in the book, that directs readers to visit your Web site. Something like this is all you need: "Hey, if you'd like to find out about even more recipes or take a peek inside our restaurant kitchens, just go to www. MyCoolRestaurantName.com and enter your name and e-mail address so we can add it to our VIP list."

I've seen other authors put their Web site URL on the bottom of the book's pages or even throughout various chapters when an example is needed or there is relevant info to be shared—it's a bit like when you see www.RockStarChef.com placed in this book.

Not all that complicated, is it? I mentioned creating a special one-page mini Web site specifically for the book. If you have used the title of your book in the Web address (URL), one of the immediate benefits is that when people search for information about you or the book, this Web site will be at the top of the page of search engine results.

You can also have people sharing this content with each other via their social media pages. What do you think happens when just a portion of those thousand book buyers I mentioned earlier engage with you or your brand in this way? Let's take a very conservative number.

Say only half of the hundred thousand customers go through and opt in at your page. That's fifty thousand or so raving enthusiastic customers who share your book page Web site with their social media friends. If the average Facebook user has 150 friends, *you* do the math… Okay, I will: 50,000 X 150 = 7,500,000.

Now, before you get all snarky on me and say there is no way ALL those people will respond and post on their Facebook wall, let's take a more realistic example and say that only half of 1 percent (0.5 percent) of the potential 7.5 million people do this. Well, guess what that number looks like: 0.5 percent of 7,500,000 = 37,500.

How much would it cost you to gain this many new fans or potential customers who have had a friend recommend that they check out your restaurant or buy your products or services? Even if you could afford to market to or contact this many people regularly through traditional media outlets (and you can't), there *is no better way* for them to hear about you or your brand than through a trusted friend.

Part of building a brand for the long haul is to be focused always on adding value and serving your customers' needs. Be a solution. Your customer dreams of a happier, less stressful, better life. Don't just sell products and services—enrich lives!

10 Reasons Why Your Web Site Sucks

If you already have your own Web site or blog, pay *special* attention to this section. If you are a large corporation or are in charge of your company's online marketing efforts, you especially need to read this section over a few times and take notes! The truth is not easy to take sometimes, and the harsh critiques that follow will only help you leave behind what isn't working, and move forward.

If a visitor clicks and lands on your Web site, you must immediately answer for them the two most important questions they are asking themselves when they arrive: ***"What is this?"*** and ***"Why do I care?"*** What will they gain from staying on your site versus the millions of other pages all vying for their attention out there on the Internet? More importantly, are you being honest and true to yourself? Does the Web site scream "Authenticity!" or does it scream "Cheesy sales tactics!"?

This book is being released in 2017. Boy, have things changed on the Internet since most of us first starting "surfing" the Web! Unfortunately, though things have gone through enormous changes, few Web sites and Web site owners have adapted and changed with the times. Having a presence on the Internet is an absolute must for any Rock Star Chef.

I spend a good portion of my Rock Star Chef Marketing Academy trainings talking about this very subject. For the purposes of this book, I'm going to highlight the most common mistakes I see on Web sites all across the Net. I'm also including blogs in this description.

Now, before you think that only small companies make these mistakes, here's the dirty little secret: some of the largest corporations I have ever consulted and worked for have made *and continue to make* these very same mistakes!

Mistake #1: It's Invisible. Have the search engines indexed any of your pages? If someone types your name or the name of your restaurant, do you come up in any of the organic listings? Do you rank for any keywords that people type into a search engine when they're looking for information? Did you set up your pages and site map correctly so that the search engines or Google's search algorithm can index you properly? Are your social media pages linked to the site? It is responsive on any device or platform?

Mistake #2: It's incomprehensible or confusing. Simple is elegant. For an example of a site that highlights simplicity, look at Apple.com.

Within milliseconds of arriving on the main page, you know just what the site is about.

Mistake #3: Your content sucks. What are you trying to accomplish by having people visit your site? Once potential customers land on your site you want them to say to themselves: "*I have found what I was looking for.*" One more thing: turn off the "auto music" that starts playing when I open a page on your site. I'm sure you're impressed with your musical selection, but I don't give a rip about your indie rock, polka favorites, or operatic overtures. Tunes are not what I'm here for.

Mistake #4: Your site is butt ugly! And not in a good way. There used to be a rallying cry in Internet marketing circles that "ugly Web sites sell." What this really meant, though, was that the less "corporate" or "slick" your Web site looked, the better it would perform, because it seemed authentic rather than sterile. But now, as more and more people have begun accessing the Web more often, users' expectations have risen. You don't need a bunch of flashy design for your site, but it should look professional, clean, and easy to navigate.

Mistake #5: It's boring. Now, I know that this may be subjective to some, but we all can agree that there is some level of expectation when we visit a site. If all the site and its owners are doing is talking about how great they are and what's the latest whiz-bang promotion they are scheduling, they've lost us. We aren't interested, and we click away from them—probably forever.

Mistake #6: Bad navigation. Your Web site must be friendly and easy to explore for all users. Increasingly, this also means mobile users. Whenever you are developing or updating your Web site, always check how it looks on a smartphone and tablet. Make sure the navigation and the other features work well for your mobile users. Remember these two important tips: **(1) Browser compatibility.** Many people surf the net with different platforms and devices. View your site in the top four: Internet Explorer, Chrome, Firefox, and Safari. Also, don't forget to check your site out on a desktop, laptop, tablet, and smartphone. (2) **Google loves "site maps,"** so make one a part of your site.

Mistake #7: It's abandoned. When was the last time you updated *any* content or information on the site? When people visit your site, is the only thing they see the new menu additions for spring 2011? (seriously, one celebrity chef did this on their site)

Mistake #8: It's broken. This is very bad juju for a Rock Star Web presence. You must be checking your site daily. And if you're *selling* any products on your site, you must have someone checking it multiple times throughout the day.

Mistake #9: It's (still) under construction. I hope this doesn't apply to you, but you'd be shocked to know how many people start a Web site and then don't do much of anything for weeks, even months. By the way, several high-profile chefs reading this right now are guilty of this very mistake. You know who you are!

Mistake #10: "Web site? We don't need no stinkin' Web site!" As hard as it is to believe, many business owners and entrepreneurs are still living with the misguided belief that having a Web site is not a necessary part of doing business today. They think that having a Web site doesn't apply to their business model, or that their customers (unlike most of the other customers in the world) aren't looking for them online. Nothing could be further from the truth. Usually, the worst reason to do something is "because everyone else is doing it." This is not the case when you are trying to sell your product or service. If you are not advertising where your competition is, you'll find yourself left behind. In the past, when your customers were looking for a product or service to fulfill a need or desire that they had, their first choice was to look in the newspaper or pull out the phone book. They would search for a store or company in the area that provided what they were looking for. Sometimes, they found only a name and phone number. Other times, they would get just an address. Rarely would they find a photo advertisement with a dynamic list of products and services offered.

Today, the experience is much different. Those same customers go to a search engine such as Google and are presented with a list of businesses that fit their needs, with links to their Web sites. Those Web pages are loaded with product pictures, videos, pricing information, maps, phone numbers, and online ordering capabilities that allow customers to order products and services *right now,* without ever having to leave their home or office.

Perhaps you have a service-oriented business that's already doing well, and you're still wondering why you should burden yourself with the added expense and effort of a Web site. Well, better wake up quick! Not having a Web site will soon be like not having a phone number that your customers can call you on. Even if your best business comes by word of mouth, your potential customers may still want to check you out online. A well-designed, professional-looking Web site will give you added visibility and credibility. And the cost of maintaining a Web site is some of the most cost effective advertising dollars you will ever spend.

Today, the Internet is one of the first places—no, make that THE FIRST PLACE—a person goes to get information.

Now, it's one thing to know you want a Web site, but it's something else altogether to know what you want your site to do for you or your customers. You must also know the difference between sales and marketing. If you are trying to have your one site be a catchall for everything and everyone, you will fail miserably. Many of the larger-brand companies have a "master site" with the many subordinate brands having a Web page or Web site all to themselves. Perhaps you want to have several sites for you, your brand, your services, your restaurants, your retail products, and so on. I cover how to set up these types of Web sites extensively in my Rock Star Chef Marketing Academy workshops.

You and Your Brand Must Have a
Digital and Social Media Presence

In addition to your main Web site, you must also have content and engagement on the main social media channels. Currently, that means Facebook, Twitter, LinkedIn and YouTube as a start. ITunes is a platform worth paying attention to, as are Pinterest, Tumblr and Instagram. The landscape and popularity of these social platforms changes just about every month. It's safe to say that if you have a presence on the main four or five (Facebook, YouTube, Twitter and LinkedIn), you will be light-years ahead of your competition.

There are many other chef- and restaurant-specific platforms and apps that I would recommend you investigate further. Do a Google search and you'll find one that matches your style and brand. It's an interesting fact to know that food, restaurants and the culinary community as a whole is one of the hottest trending verticals in the New Digital Economy. The Best-In-Class platform that I have seen specifically for chefs and other culinary professionals is Chef's Roll. You can visit them at www.ChefsRoll.com and sign up for a free basic profile. In a short amount of time, ChefsRoll.com has become the hub for all sorts of media, agency and industry interest. Casting directors from Food Network, Top Chef and Hell's Kitchen have found amazing talent on this site. Investors and hiring managers are increasingly using the site to fund talented chefs in new food ventures and several high profile restaurant and hotel gigs have been awarded to the roster of chefs. Several brand ambassadors, culinary consultants and foodservice brands have used Chef's Roll for integrated marketing campaigns. In full disclosure, I am a strategic advisor to Chef's Roll and will be working with them on an on-going basis in the future. Chef's Roll was created specifically for chefs as a way to showcase their talent, artistry and uniqueness. It's often referred to as *"LinkedIn for Chefs"*.

The world of social media has exploded. It seems as thought every week a "new" social media app or site hits the market. The problem with most of these sites, is that they are not focused. In other words, they exist to encapsulate all topics. That is good and sometimes better, but some people may prefer a network that is dedicated to one topic. After all, if you are passionate about one thing, everything else can be noise.

This is particularly true of chefs -- we are passionate people that dedicate ourselves to preparing, cooking and presenting amazing food. While a site like Facebook could store pictures of meals and cooking techniques, there is a good chance that it will be lost among the sea of cat videos, Kim Kardashian's butt and chain letters. And so, Chef's Roll has been born…it's a platform where chefs can tell the full story of their culinary life, both visually and through the written word, through a simple online tool: a Facebook-LinkedIn-Craigslist hybrid, but with more bells and whistles. It brings a chef's career goals within reach by providing a clean, succinct and beautiful platform for sharing the breadth of their culinary story.

"The quality of a chef's online presence almost never matches the quality of their cuisine. Thus, we're building the largest professional chef network in the world, where chefs are able to promote their talent, career achievements, unique style and more through this interactive, cost-effective and sophisticated tool. Chef's Roll was developed out of our respect for chefs and what they do best", says Chef's Roll co-founder Thomas Keslinke.

The social network explains some of the things chefs can share:

- Skills and expertise
- Upcoming events
- Education and experience
- A synopsis of the type of cuisine they specialize in
- Photos and videos

- Awards and accolades
- Client reviews
- Links to print online and television press

Again, visit them at ChefsRoll.com or on Facebook and become part of the community.

Overall, the share of adult U.S. Internet users who have a profile on at least one social networking site has risen dramatically over the past five years—from 8 percent in 2005 to 35 percent in 2008, to 67 percent in 2015. For adults aged 18–29, it's 72 percent, and for teens it's 82 percent (in other words, just about everybody).

There's also a fundamental change in people using social networks from mobile devices rather than desktops. More and more mobile Web users (91 percent of them) are using it to socialize, compared to the only 79 percent of desktop users who access social media. It appears that the mobile phone is actually a better platform than the PC for social networking. Who knew?

It can be tough to focus on what is working and what is the latest cool platform that customers are engaging with. And it's only going to get more and more confusing as the popularity of these platforms increases. To find out the ones I am recommending now, visit www.ChefMarkGarcia.com.

Video Rock Star

Video on the Web continues to grow and grow and must be a keystone of your Rock Star Chef personal branding. YouTube is part of the cultural landscape, and you MUST have a video presence online. I was just at a party in New York City, hosted by a company that was introducing its strategy for the next few years. If anyone has *any* doubt that YouTube is well on its way to becoming a media company, this is your wake up call! Jay-Z was the featured performer, and many other media brands were in attendance or performing as well. YouTube is courting just about every segment of media to create "channel sequencing" to rival any network or media company. Other services, such as Wistia, Viddler and Vimeo, are all great avenues to promote your videos. Whether or not those videos are on your own Web site or on a "channel" that you have created, video is a crucial part to becoming a Rock Star Chef.

A nice benefit is that the search engines LOVE video and will give you lots of juice for your rankings when you have video content. Do a video search for Rock Star Chef Mark Garcia on Google and see who, curiously, comes up.

During my Rock Star Chef Marketing Masters program, I go into deep-dive detail about the video process. We spend time showing you proven tips and techniques in a step-by-step process that will help you dominate the Web with your videos! You can find information about the program in the resource section. I also have a DVD program that takes you through the entire process of creating effective video segments that get tons of traffic for you or your brands.

Insider Secrets of the Profitable "P's": Positioning, Packaging, and PR

The ultimate and overriding goal of the three "P's" is to help you achieve rock star status by becoming a recognized brand, expert, or both. You can't leave the perception of you or your company up to the customer— they'll almost always draw the wrong conclusion. You must define who you are and what you wish to be known for so that the media can tell your story for you.

People buy those things and frequent those places that are interesting, intriguing, real, and emotional and that have social proof. Positioning and packaging gives all those things. It is your primary responsibility to tell your customers and fans what to think about you or your service, and to do all you can to be sure they are thinking of you as often as possible. Remember, to stand out as a Rock Star Chef, you must be relevant, frequent, and memorable.

Here's a list of inexpensive ways to promote yourself or your joint:

- **Do publicity stunts.** (These require great planning and creativity. Make sure you have permitting in place if necessary.)
- **Have contests** (on your social media sites).
- **Give awards** (on your social media sites).
- **Host your own radio program** (online or traditional).
- **Host your own TV show** (online or traditional cable).
- **Blog** (both on a blog and on social media sites).
- **Become a published author.**
- **Write and submit articles for publication.**
- **Speak.**
- **Adopt a non-profit or charity organization that speaks to your heart.**
- **Be a guest on local morning radio and TV shows.**

The Rock Star Chef System Revealed: Developing Your Personal Brand Successfully Online

My Internet marketing mentor, Ken McCarthy, sums it up pretty simply. To make money consistently on the Internet, all you need to know is the following equation:

$$\text{Traffic} + \text{Conversion} = \text{Profit}$$

Short, simple, and to the point! Ken has always had a way of taking complex ideas and concepts and distilling them down to their essence. In the first wave of Internet marketing, to be successful and make money all you had to do was drive visitors (**traffic**) to your Web site, give them a compelling offer (**conversion**) that enticed them to pull out their credit cards, and—voila! —**profit.**

Well, things have gotten a bit more complicated and expensive these days in Web 3.0. Traffic and conversion are still critical to online success, but because online advertising (OLA) has become a huge business, you simply can't ignore those costs as we did back in the day when we were buying pay-per-clicks at a nickel or ten cents a pop!

My other Internet marketing mentor, Perry Marshall adds another brilliant indicator to the equation. The variable added to the **Traffic + Conversion** equation is *Economics.* What do I mean by this? The triangle below illustrates that in order to sell something, you have to get **traffic;** then you have to **convert** that traffic; and **economics** means you have a process in place to turn a profit on what you sell—which is why you are in business in the first place.

If you can make a profit, then you can reinvest in getting more **traffic** and **converting** that traffic and further improving your **economics**... and on an on it goes in a circular fashion. It's a process and framework for how to make money in the New Digital Economy.

Traffic + Conversion + Economics = Profit

This framework can be summed up in 3 simple steps:

1. *Who* would purchase this product or service? (That's **T.**)
2. Can you reach this audience *affordably* and *efficiently*? (That's **E.**)
3. Does your marketing message *persuade* them to buy? (That's **C.**)

Copyright 2017
Perry S. Marshall & Associates

A word of caution, though: *simple* doesn't mean *easy*, and there is more to that little triangular framework above than there is space in this book to cover it. Each side of the equation has its own set of rules, techniques, and guidelines. You can buy all the traffic you can afford, but if the Web sites or social platforms you send that traffic to aren't relevant to your potential customers, they will be gone in the blink of an eye (or the click of a mouse). Your dollars spent have now channeled hordes of people to your Web properties, and they did not take the action(s) that you hoped. How long do you think you can afford to be doing that activity?

This is why I am so passionate about teaching you how to get that traffic to take the actions you desire (conversion), so that both you and the customer are happy with the transaction. Economics comes into play so that you can continue to sustain the message/marketing campaign.

There are several examples of how to create and execute this kind of campaign throughout this book, and in just a moment I am going to give you a real-world example. The key thing I want you to understand is that you must put equal effort into *creating the messaging* and *testing the results* for your online campaigns. We cover this process extensively in my marketing workshops.

Branding 101—Rock Star Chef Style

How you develop your personal brand is the key to monetizing your passions on the Internet. It doesn't matter if you are delivering your content via video, podcasts, blog, or articles—the ***authentic you*** is the one and only thing that will separate you from everyone else. Besides, do you really think you're the only chef or restaurateur reading this book or attending one of my marketing trainings?

There are going to be plenty of entrepreneurs and chefs who begin to build their Rock Star Chef brand, and that is a good thing!

What will separate you from them is YOU! There is only one of you, and the sooner you realize that your business and your personal brand are one and the same, the easier it will be to become a true Rock Star Chef.

Monetizing a personal brand is nothing new, and it isn't rocket science. Think of Emeril, Wolfgang, and Martha Stewart. They built their empires by being who they are and never backing down. We are lucky that they blazed a trail before us and allowed a new era of publishing and promoting to take place.

What is new and exciting is that this first generation of Rock Star Chefs built their brands on TV, radio, magazines, and newspapers and were confined by cost, distribution, and tightly controlled platforms.

The new breed will do it online, at a much cheaper cost, ten times faster. And, most importantly of all, they will accomplish all this without the need for a gatekeeper's approval or permission.

Are you thinking of trying to get your own cooking show approved by a cable station or network such as Food Network, the Cooking Channel, FOX, or Bravo? F*@k that! Create your own TV show with any of the many online video outlets (both live and prerecorded), gain an audience, get advertisers, create affiliate commissions, and I promise you that you will pique the interest of those national shows—who will start coming to *you* to talk about a production deal.

"Where the eyeballs go, the Benjamin's flow!"

Here is a quick overview of what the process looks like. Let's say you love Spanish olive oil and you happen to know a ton about the stuff. It's almost *embarrassing* how much you love to talk about Spanish olive oil. At cocktail parties you find yourself talking to the staff because you quickly overwhelmed every guest you met, with your passion for

Spanish olive oil. Now, you might be saying to yourself that passion is good, but how exactly do you make money on this knowledge?

Simple: you use the Internet to create a platform where you can talk about Spanish olive oil till you are blue in the face. Here's a curious thing about passion: it can become very contagious! When you learn to channel that passion into creating amazing content, and distribute that content via social media tools, fellow enthusiasts will find you. One of those enthusiasts who is a thought leader or person of influence will hear you say, *"Spanish olive oils have a certain aphrodisiac quality to them, and that's why so many Spanish men and women enjoy a wildly fulfilling sex life into their nineties."* And he or she will sense a business opportunity and reach out to you.

The two of you may brainstorm and create an online video channel (YouTube), blog (Tumblr), or podcast (iTunes) around your passion to reach the olive oil consumer marketplace. The content is launched, and olive oil enthusiasts are drawn to you and your passion. You build a community using all the social media tools (Facebook, Twitter, and Pinterest) and techniques you are learning here. You bust your butt working *on* the business and not *in* it, and you keep your laser focus on serving and engaging your community.

Out of nowhere, one of the biggest Spanish olive oil importers asks to advertise on the site. The Spanish Olive Oil Commission asks to place social links to your site (which boosts your Google page rank tremendously). You keep adding relevant content, building up your community, and start to create additional revenue streams, and all of a sudden, your passion is making you money.

Now you know why I stress the opportunity that exists now that never did before for the small entrepreneur. Easy access and the tremendous reach of social media tools, coupled with low cost of entry, means that anyone willing to WORK can do this. Remember that you are building a brand and creating a name for yourself or your business.

By the way, the above scenario I just described happens EVERY DAY in the food world. Many of the chefs mentioned in the beginning of this book, as well as some of my celebrity chef clients, were able to get their branded products into the marketplace in a very similar fashion.

Here's the Recipe

This is a quick checklist of tasks that must be completed for the above Spanish olive oil example. You can use this template as you build your personal brand.

1. Identify your passion.
2. Create relevant content about your passion (articles, videos, social media posts and so on).
3. Create your brand or tagline.
4. Buy your brand name, personal name, restaurant name, book name, or tagline domain name (otherwise known as a URL). (go daddy affiliate link)
5. Decide on the medium you feel most comfortable with (video, written word, audio, or a combination of all three).
6. Create a WordPress or Tumblr blog. (affiliate link)
7. Create social media accounts (Google+, Facebook, YouTube, Twitter, LinkedIn, Pinterest).
8. Post relevant and engaging content regularly.
9. Engage in the community by being a contributor, not a salesperson.
10. Rinse and repeat.

Voila! You are on your way.

Yes, You DO Need to Create a Media Kit

There are tons of books and articles on the Internet about what the media outlets want in a press kit or media package. As you begin the process of building your personal brand, the media will contact you. It's not a matter of *if*; it's a matter of *when*—and the *when* comes sooner than you think.

Trust me on this: you want to be prepared when a media outlet wants to do a story on you or your business. There is no worse feeling in the world than being asked by a reporter or show producer for your media kit or at least a professional head shot photo…and not having one. What most people do in this situation is grab a picture (that looks horrible) off the computer and send it to the requesting person. Rock Star Chefs DO NOT do this—ever!

I'm going to give you what I have used with clients in the past. It has generated lots of exposure for them or their places of business. You should have both an online and an off-line media kit available. When your online media kit is easily identifiable on one of your Web sites, an interested party can download all the materials and digital assets right away. Make it easy for them to find by labeling the page "Press Kit" or "Press Info" or "Media Page".

Your media kits should contain the following:

- Your media release and pitch letter
- A high quality, clear photo of you, your place of business, your unique service or your product(s)—Have both a Hi-Res and Low-Res copy available
- A PDF file of your media release, and copies of any of your promo materials (TV appearances, events, press clippings, radio spots, and so on)
- Business info (think address, phone number, e-mail, and so on)

- A list of frequently asked questions (FAQ's) or questions you would *like* to be asked
- A short video or audio of you in action (could be a simple interview or presentation from your iPhone's video camera, or an audio file)
- Best way to get in touch with you QUICKLY (for writers, reporters, and producers on a deadline who need to speak to you right away…as in answer your phone on the third ring!)
- A Culinary POV or I Believe video. Your customers and future customers want to engage and get to know the "real" you. In today's digital world people want to relate to authentic people. I recommend creating a short 5-7 minute video where you share in a very personable and casual way why you do what you do or think the way you do. This is something I have recently shared with my high level coaching and consulting clients and they are having tremendous success with this. Feel free to use mine as an example at www.CheMarkGarcia.com.

Build Your Brigade

The great thing about online marketing is that it has never been easier for an individual chef, product producer, or small restaurateur to compete with the big boys on a national scale. We cover this subject extensively in my multiday marketing boot camp, but I want to give you a glimpse of this powerful tool. Would it surprise you to know there is a way for you to create your own hungry legion of fans who want to tell the world how great you are? And these fans also want to help you market your goods and services!

Affiliates and an affiliate marketing program are what I am talking about. Don't worry if you think you've never heard about this before—you probably have participated in this scenario and didn't even know it.

Have you ever been to a Web site and clicked on a link or banner ad that took you to another site, where you bought a product or service? Well, that, my friend, is a very simplified example of an affiliate program. The original site you were on was paid a commission on your purchase and, depending on the program, will get a commission for any other products you may buy this year or the next.

Amazon.com and eBay are great examples of businesses that have a tremendous affiliate program. Some of the largest retailers use affiliate programs on the Internet with their vendor partners. They pay people to put links on their Web sites, comment on blogs, and even send out e-mails that have special codes or links embedded in them. Every time a sale gets rung up, both parties receive income from the transaction. This is a great way for Rock Star Chefs to get the word out about themselves, their business, or their products.

Make Your Marketing Work

There's an old saying that the key to success in real estate investing is "location, location, location." Another saying is that most successful businesses will agree that half their marketing is working really well for them—they just don't know which half! In marketing, the key to identifying and tracking success is to "test, test, and test."

What should you test? How about everything! Well, everything *important.* Don't test silly things like blue envelopes versus yellow envelopes (if you are mailing). Test the big things that matter on any of your marketing material. Whether your marketing is online or off-line, you should test in this order:

1. Headline
2. Opening sentence or paragraph
3. Your close (often the "P.S." in a sales letter)
4. Your offer or call to action (CTA)

5. Body copy
6. Ad size
7. Graphics or pictures

The Supreme Power of Split Testing

One way to test your advertising is by running what is called a *split test* or *A/B splits*. Almost any magazine, newspaper, or Web site will offer this inexpensive method of testing.

Essentially, you are running two different headlines, and the platform you are running off will run half with one headline or ad, and half with the other headline or ad. This is the most scientific kind of advertising testing available. You will often be surprised by the results and data that you get when you split test. Sometimes, one subtle change of a word will cause one ad or headline to out-pull another significantly.

Once you find your control ad or headline keep it until something beats it! When you are split testing, you are always testing against a control. That control is your best ad, headline, or marketing piece up to now.

Only after comparing results will you make any changes. DON'T GUESS what your market wants—**ASK IT!** Let the customers cast their votes with dollars and responses.

In advertising, keep doing what works. Never, ever change what is working unless you've found something that works better. This is a deceptively simple concept, but one that many smart, big-budget advertisers screw up royally and repeatedly. As soon as an ad or other marketing piece starts to work, everybody wants to change it. It doesn't matter if your spouse, girlfriend, or staff "wants to see something new"—don't do it! Your customers and the marketplace will tell you when it's not working anymore. Some of the best ads have been running for twenty years or more and still out-pull every new test ad.

Remember, you are not advertising and promoting to a static marketplace. You are marketing to a constantly moving parade of *individuals*. Because people's needs and wants keep changing, your job is to be a consistent marketer who attracts and maintains current and new clients, customers, and business.

Key Ingredients in Your Recipe for Success

- Key Ingredients in Your Recipe for Success
- Welcome to Web 3.0. It's responsive, it's social and it's mobile. Are you prepared?
- Build Your Brand Online. Capture e-mails and opt-in information.
- Web sites: *What is this, and why should I care?* Check out Apple. com, BMW.com, RGA.com and Nike.com
- Social media presence: you must be on Facebook, Twitter, LinkedIn, YouTube, Pinterest, Instagram and Google+.
- Think video, video, and video.
- Find affiliates—or, better yet, help them find *you*.
- Split Test all of your major marketing messaging.

CHAPTER 8

LIKE-MINDED INDIVIDUALS

"I like to start my day off with a glass of Champagne. I like to wind it up with Champagne, too. To be frank, I also like a glass or two in between. It may not be the universal medicine for every disease... but it does you less harm than just about any other liquid."

—**Fernand Point**

The Power of a Mastermind

We become like those we most associate with. Our parents knew this powerful principle, and the success gurus will tell you that you, my friend, are the sum total of the five closest friends you hang out with. What's even spookier is that if you were to average up the annual salary of that same close circle of friends, your current annual income would be within 10 percent of that number.

Now, I don't bring this up as a negative, nor am I trying to suggest that you get yourself a whole new roster of friends, but I am trying to illustrate the power—good or bad—of your closest social circle, and how that influences your current level of success or the lack thereof.

Being an entrepreneur for as long as I have has brought me many highs—and plenty of lows, too. When I left corporate America the first time to venture out on my own, many of my close friends and colleagues thought I was stark raving mad to leave the "security" of a high-paying job and strike out on my own. They warned me all about the perils of "working without a net." I, on the other hand, thought *they* were the crazy ones to stay in an environment that did not allow them to control their time, destiny, or earning potential.

Besides, "job security" was an oxymoron in my book. Early in my career I had seen too many corporate layoffs, downsizings, "rightsizings," job description re-scoping and company implosions where good people were hurt by the greedy, self-serving executives in charge. Remember Enron, or WorldCom anybody? How about the banks and insurance companies from *Too Big to Fail*?

Throughout most of my adult life, I have been involved in some way with a mastermind group. Especially when I ventured out on my own, how could I talk about the challenges and problems I was facing as an entrepreneur, with the Dilberts still stuck in Cubicle Nation? Their daily challenges and mine were utterly, wildly different.

So I had to find a group of fellow entrepreneurs and business owners who knew intimately what I was going through. We shared business challenges and successes with each other. We also bounced new marketing ideas and revenue generators off each other. Even though each of us may have been in a completely different business arena, what we collectively brought to the group was more powerful and insightful than what any one of us could ever have done on our own.

Over the years, my mastermind group has changed based on the direction my business is heading. Each year or so, I join or create a new group of like-minded individuals, depending on the challenges I am currently experiencing. Sometimes, members of previous mastermind groups join my new ones if they are venturing into the same world I am. I have maintained many of my Internet marketing mastermind colleagues for several years.

The Power of Coaches and Mentors

In addition to the mastermind group principle, I have always believed in the benefit of hiring coaches and mentors for my personal and professional life. When we were young and growing up, this seemed so natural for us. Think of all the coaches, trainers, and instructors you had who taught you new things. As you grew up, these influential people continued to hone the skills you had learned, and pushed you to become better and better.

But for some reason, as we get older we tend to dismiss the benefit of having these individuals in our lives, and I'm not sure why that is. Perhaps it's because we are afraid to admit that we need help. Or, worse yet, we delude ourselves into thinking we can do it on our own. Not only is that kind of thinking dangerous, it's also downright dumb!

Having coaches doesn't always mean they are *better* than we are at what we're trying to learn how to do. Do you really think that any basketball coach Michael Jordan ever had was a better player than he was? What about Tiger Woods? When he hired a swing coach to change his swing midway through his career, do you think the coach he had could drive a golf ball farther than Tiger? And do you suppose any of Muhammad Ali's trainer's could go five rounds with him in the ring? *Of course not!* These coaches all helped bring out the potential and genius that these superstars had inside them. They taught them not only the mechanics of their game but also the mind-set necessary to achieving success.

I have several coaches currently and will always invest in myself to have such valuable individuals help propel me quickly toward my goals and dreams.

Get an Accountability Partner

This principle has served me fully as well as my mastermind groups have over the years. What I mean by an accountability partner is someone you meet with regularly for just a few minutes to go over goals you have set for yourself, and projects you have attached a deadline to.

This person doesn't even have to be directly involved with what you are doing in your business. It's nice if they have some idea of what you're doing, but their main focus and benefit to you is that every week you will be meeting with them for fifteen minutes or so and updating them on your progress with the tasks you set for yourself the last time you spoke. When you know that each week you will be meeting with someone who isn't your boss or taskmaster and whom you will have to update on what you've been doing, something magical starts to happen.

You will be amazed to see how hard you strive to get things done because you know that you are meeting your accountability partner. Sometimes, you will strive harder to avoid letting down the other person than you ever would have if you had only yourself to answer to. It's human nature: we want to please others and not let them down. Try it for a month or so, and see if you don't agree with me.

Key Ingredients in Your Recipe for Success

- Key Ingredients in Your Recipe for Success
- Power of a mastermind—try it and you'll never try to go it alone again.

- Coaches and mentors—be mindful whom you listen to.
- Accountability partners—they bring out your A game.
- The master is always a student first—you should be constantly seeking new ideas.

CHAPTER 9

ALWAYS GIVE BACK

"A good dinner is of great importance to good conversation. One cannot think well, love well, sleep well, if one has not dined well."
—**Virginia Woolf**

Think Globally, Act Locally

As chefs, restaurateurs, or food service professionals, when it comes to supporting worthwhile causes we have a vast array of choices in front of us. I can think of no other industry that has so many avenues for us to lend our support. Food is a basic human need, and the entire process, from seed to farm to table, has dedicated organizations that want to affect the world in meaningful ways. In the resource section of this book, you can find out about the nonprofit organizations that I am involved with.

I'm not suggesting that any organization you decide to get involved with has to be centered on food. There are many, many worthwhile causes that have nothing at all to do with food. I would just suggest that you find a cause that you are passionate about or want to increase awareness of. When you dedicate a portion of your time and resources to worthwhile causes, you can and will make a difference in your community.

There is no greater feeling in the world than that of associating yourself with like-minded individuals and a charity that is trying to make the world a better place. Besides, one of the keystones to success is to serve others. I know of no individual or corporation who has experienced lasting financial success without giving back and serving others. It's just the way it all works!

Chefs Bring Cachet to Events and Fundraisers

One of the first "celebrity chefs" I worked with early in my career taught me the power of getting involved with charity events and fund-raisers. Not only is it fun and wonderfully satisfying to the soul, but it also can be a great way to get the word out about yourself, your business, and your brand.

This mentor of mine gets involved locally in the Atlanta area where he lives. He's not only done the traditional committee or chair volunteer positions, but he has also become an emcee for events, where those in attendance get a taste of his personality and style and, of course, learn about his business as well. One of the most extraordinary things he did was to run for a local government board position. When he ran for this office, he was able to put up campaign signs (with his name and personal brand) legally all over his community. How smart is *that*?

Chefs and restaurateurs have become mini celebrities over the past few years. It's a cool gig to have since everyone knows what food is, and has probably eaten in a restaurant where the food was prepared by a chef or cook. I don't think every profession on the planet can say that just about everybody is intimately familiar with what they do and has consumed or experienced their craft. Also, the chef has a rich history, and food customs are a part of *everyone's* culture and history. You as the chef or restaurateur will bring a natural flair, or Rock Star Chef cachet, to any event that you are associated with.

Food Nourishes the Soul

One of the many ways you can help your local community is to sponsor an event with free or discounted food. People will associate the good feelings they get from helping out a charity or event with the food you provide. Many times, you have a captive audience that you can market to or get contact info from to add to your list of fans.

You could also sponsor a local soup kitchen or food bank with money, products, or volunteer time. This is a great venue for you to pass on to the younger generations of chefs and cooks just how great an impact they can make by sharing a little of their time and expertise in a kitchen that doesn't normally see this caliber of volunteer.

These organizations are always looking for donations of food to fill their pantries. Unfortunately, as you and I both know, ours is an industry that tends to waste prodigious amounts of food and ingredients. If we had an outlet for that excess, think of all the hungry mouths we could feed!

Life's Too Short for a Bad Meal

One of my favorite ways to get involved in fund-raising for a charity is at the silent-auction dinner or brunch that many organizations have during the year. Working with the organizers of the event, I would put together a visiting chef's dinner in the private home of the auction winner. We would decide on a predetermined number of guests and auction off a dinner to the highest bidder. Sometimes, we included wine; sometimes, we didn't. I would volunteer my time, and I would get other chefs or caterers to volunteer staff so that we could professionally cook and serve a gourmet dinner in the home of the auction winner.

I would get my local food suppliers to donate the needed ingredients and supplies. That way, a larger portion of the bid price would go to the charity. This was always one of the highest-grossing and most popular auction items because it was an *experience.*

The auction winner would invite over friends, family, business colleagues, or sometimes employees to partake in this intimate experience of having a professional chef turn their home into a hot-spot restaurant for the evening.

Can you imagine the personal branding touches that a Rock Star Chef could have with an event like this? Besides, with the popularity of social media sites and the general popularity of smartphones, attendees at these events can live "tweet" and update their Facebook profiles about the great food experience they are enjoying with this fantastic Rock Star Chef!

Now You Have a Friend in the Restaurant Business

You should want to give back to your local community by donating time and money to charities that you are passionate about. There should be no expectation on your part to have anything come back to you other than a satisfying feeling of doing good for others.

You'll make friends by being involved with these organizations and the people who associate with them. Being a chef is a high-profile, fun job to have. Of course, when you give in this way many folks will naturally want to associate with you and your business, and that's always a good thing.

Key Ingredients in Your Recipe for Success

- Key Ingredients in Your Recipe for Success
- Get involved in your community by sponsoring or volunteering with those organizations that resonate with you personally.
- Stay involved with those organizations. They desperately need consistent supporters who believe in them and in the positive impact they are making in the community.
- Each year, build a line item into your budget where you will donate 10% of your income/revenue to a worthy organization. Not only will a deserving organization get funds that they desperately need, watch what happens to you and/or your organization when you contribute positive JuJu to the universe.
- As chefs and culinary professionals, we have been blessed to have a voice and platform in not only pop culture, but the larger social community as well. I challenge you to take this newfound notoriety and stage to help move the conversation forward in improving the ways in which we grow, harvest, process and ultimately serve food in our communities.

CHAPTER 10

CHOICES: MAKE INTELLIGENT ONES

"A gourmet who thinks of calories is like a tart who looks at her watch."

—James Beard

Choose Your Thoughts Carefully

To achieve Rock Star Chef status, you must get rid of the negative thoughts and excuses you may have allowed yourself to make in the past, and instead focus on the *solutions* to what you want to achieve in your life going forward. Get over the "mañana syndrome." Quit being an "I've got to" person, and become an "I get to" person. Quit *talking* about doing things and actually get them done! Every excuse you give yourself or let others give you will lend substance to your failures or perceived challenges, making them that much more real. You can be the victim, or you can be the victor. It's your choice.

Every day, it seems, a new article or study comes out describing how the human brain is the most amazing supercomputer on the planet. Each year, we learn more and more about how both our conscious and subconscious mind determine both who we are and the results we are getting in our lives. I love reading the many great authors and experts on this subject. Now, I'm not talking about all that "think positive and everything will magically go your way" b.s. Quite the contrary. As we learn more about how the brain works and how we can access its true potential, the possibilities are endless. You can use some very simple techniques and habits to harness the power of this amazing creation. If you're ready to take your game to the next level and accomplish more in the next few months than most people will manage in a lifetime, then read on.

Here are four strategies that I and other successful entrepreneurs have used effectively time and time again:

1. Choose your self-talk. Thoughts are things. You are programming your unconscious mind with everything you put into it. It doesn't reject or analyze; it just absorbs. If you constantly tell yourself negative things, you are systematically programming yourself for failure. You're too good for that. Conversely, if you feed your subconscious mind with *positive* thoughts, images, and phrases, you are setting yourself up for success. Program yourself constantly with gratitude, positive affirmations, and positive thoughts. When you find yourself saying "I can't" or other negative, defeatist things, say to yourself, "Cancel, cancel," and change the phrase to "I *will*." You'll be amazed at how this simple technique will change your outlook and results in just a few days.

2. Choose your environment. There are certain people in your life who are sucking the life and energy from you. These are the folks telling you that you can't do something. They have negative comments about everyone and everything: the economy, the press, their job, even their family and friends. They just can't accept that anything worthwhile is achievable or attainable. I use the term "toxic people" to describe these folks. They are forever moaning and complaining and can never find anything good or positive in any situation. If it's a beautiful day outside, they are the ones complaining that the bright sunshine will force them to wear shades. I have an interesting perspective on these individuals: they are jealous or insecure about your forward momentum.

Who are the people you choose to let into your life? Whom do you surround yourself with? Do they support unconditionally the dreams and aspirations that you cherish? Even though they may not always fully understand what you are trying to do, do they value it because it's important to you? Are they adding value to your life? Not that you should put a price tag on what they bring to the table, but make sure they aren't like those crabs in the boiling pot: pulling down any of their fellows that try to climb out. Statistically, your net worth and income will become the average of the five people you spend the most time with.

What peer group do you interact with? Are the folks you network with playing at the level you wish to engage at? Who is your competition? Play against people who are better than you. They will make you stretch and grow in ways that others can't. Besides, million-dollar ideas sometimes come from the challenge of playing with folks who are at a different level from yours.

3. Choose to focus on your self-worth. Before you can ever be a cheerleader for someone else, you must learn to be one for yourself. All too often, we put other people's dreams, ambitions, and goals ahead of ours. Now, I'm not suggesting you become a self-centered jerk or some high-maintenance diva, but I am going to suggest that you take time and focus your thoughts and actions on what you want to do on your chosen career path. You can't always let others impose their will on you. Focus on your passions and what makes you happy. To thine own self be true.

4. Choose your event outcomes. As you journey on your path to Rock Star Chef status, one inescapable truth that you will probably appreciate sooner rather than later is, *shit happens!* Sorry to be so blunt, but you were bound to learn this cosmic truth anyway. We may not always be able to control or predict the events that happen in life, but the one thing we can control is our *response* to those events. Good or bad, right or wrong, take comfort in knowing that most of what happens in life is directly dependent, not on what happens to you, but on how you respond to it. Think of it this as a simple math equation:

$$E + R = O$$

"**E**" stands for "events." Events happen, and you can't always control events that happen in life. The only thing you *can* control is your reaction or response (the "**R**") to the events that happen in your life. This reaction or response will directly influence the outcome (the "**O**") of the event.

Bonus Strategy: Choose to be a servant leader. There are several books on the subject that do a better job than I ever could of explaining to you all the nuances of this trait. Suffice it to say that any Rock Star Chef I work with has at his or her core, in their very DNA, the desire to serve others and add value to their lives before they ever think of benefiting themselves. When you are living and leading a life in this manner, the universe just seems to open up to you in amazing ways.

Practice Doesn't Always Make Perfect

Many of the habits, actions, and choices you make to become successful in business and in life come down to simple discipline. While the actions themselves are not all that complicated, you still must act consistently and without distraction. Step-by-step achievement is the craft for Rock Star Chefs.

Don't focus solely on the process; focus on the end result. If you focus only on the day-to-day process, it's not always going to be fun. You are going to feel uncomfortable, you may get bored, you might become frustrated, and you will most certainly get tired at times. Remind yourself that correct actions become correct habits, which turn into correct outcomes.

Choose to Face Adversity Head-On

Adversity has thrown a monkey wrench into many a young entrepreneur's or business owner's dreams of success. Get used to the fact that adversity is part of the game. Don't let it paralyze you with inaction. To do nothing is to roll over and accept defeat. Don't. Instead, DO SOMETHING. You accomplish more through movement than you ever will with meditation. You can't just wish that something would happen. You can't get in shape if you don't start eating better and going to the gym. You can't create an empire online if you don't learn how to set up the right kinds of Web sites and marketing campaigns.

Fear creeps into the mind and paralyzes us into not taking action. We fear failure, or we fear that when we try something new we might not be very good at it, and *blah, blah, blah!* We are born with two fears: fear of falling and fear of loud noises. Besides those two, most people have further burdened themselves with other fears that they learned or conditioned themselves with.

Creating the right action will move you forward when adversity or challenge rises up in your path to becoming a Rock Star Chef. Think back to when you first learned how to ride a bike. The more you kept getting up and getting back on the bike, the easier it got. Think about the first cooking job you had. Were you scared as hell that first Friday night on the line as the chef was calling out tickets to you? Continue to face your fears and overcome them.

Five Key Steps to Getting Back Up
When Life Knocks You Down

1. Choose the right attitude. You have to choose the right attitude about yourself and your path. Mind-set, attitude, or perspective—call it what you want. How you choose to see yourself is also how others will see you. When you wake up in the morning you have a choice in how you see the day. Nothing positive comes from focusing on the negative. It's your choice. You need to expect great things to come out of you. Although, as the song says, you can't always get what you want, you generally do get what you *expect*. It's what you absolutely believe and are ready for that matters.

2. Take action on any adversity that shows up in your life. If you don't, adversity will take action on you and beat you down. That's when negative talk starts to rear its ugly head. And as I have said before, thoughts are things, and you don't want negative talk starting to compound itself inside your head. You fail in life only if you quit or give up.

One of the greatest feel-good movies ever made is *Rudy*, the true story of Rudy Ruttager. This man knew how to overcome challenges! He dreamed of playing on the Notre Dame football team even though coaches, friends, family, and fellow players all told him it would never come true. Even though he was assigned to the practice team only, Rudy never gave up on his dream of actually playing on the field in a real, live Notre Dame game. What we can learn from him is that if the dream is big enough and strong enough in you, the obstacle doesn't matter. Nothing comes from focusing on the negative—yes, be aware of it, but don't *focus* on it.

I had a chance to hear the personal story of how Rudy accomplished this particular dream and the follow-up dream of actually getting a real Hollywood studio to make his story into a feature-length movie. Let me tell you, after hearing him talk about all the rejection, humiliation, and negative feedback he had heard over and over for years while he was trying to achieve his dreams…well, you or I can NEVER AGAIN get away with complaining or feeling sorry for ourselves because someone initially shoots down our ideas or goals. I mean, this guy suffered through put-downs, smack–downs, and plain old ridicule about just why he would never accomplish his dreams and why he should just give up because no way in hell was he ever going to make them happen. Well, thankfully, Rudy had a different plan in mind, and he didn't pay attention to all the people telling him he couldn't do what he knew in his heart and soul he was GOING to do! The speech was one of the most awe-inspiring stories I have ever heard. Look him up online and see if you don't agree.

3. Take the "t" out of "can't." Realistic ambitions can be achieved. Find a way to get it done. Ask yourself one question: *What do I (or we) have to do to make it happen?* Do the best you can with the hand that you are dealt. It's not that you *can't;* you just haven't yet figured out how to do it.

4. Don't fall victim to the "if only" disease. Don't blame your circumstances on people, situations, or the cruel hand of fate. Take responsibility for where you are in your life at this moment. You get what you put out. That's the law of attraction, also known as karma.

5. Remember that rejection isn't a permanent state. Dr. Seuss got rejected twenty-seven times before he sold his first book. But he believed in himself, and he knew that a rejection was not some sort of final judgment from the universe. So he didn't quit. And he sold over two million books, along with winning two Academy Awards, two Emmys, a Pulitzer Prize, and a Peabody Award. Don't use rejection as an excuse to quit. Focus on the solutions, not the excuses.

Choose to Be a Goal *Doer*, Not Just a Goal Setter: The Seven-Step Plan

The traditional wisdom and teaching from the recent past is just to set goals in your life and everything will work out. Well, there's a missing piece to that equation, and that is actually how to *achieve* those goals. Setting goals is a great thing, and I think everyone should, but if you aren't careful, goals can be nothing more than empty wishes. Rock Star Chefs constantly remind themselves, "I will achieve this!" The law of attraction comes into play. Sometimes we fear success. Why? Because when you are successful, people watch you more. There is a ton of pressure not only to achieve but also to maintain the goals and achievements we have set for ourselves. Why are goals are so important? Simple: *so you don't have any regrets at the end of your life!*

The Real Recipe for Goal Achievement: Goal Doing

Step 1. Have specific goals for the different areas of your life. For example; you can't just say, "I want to make more money." That's too general. Be more specific! "I want to make an extra $100K this year. I will make an extra hundred thousand dollars in income by March 15 of next year." Your subconscious mind comes into play and goes to work on the task.

I've listed below some of the key areas that I have used in my own journey of achievement. I hope this list will help spark some ideas for your own goals list. All the information you could ever want is out there. Do you want to achieve more in your life? Well, the answers are out there! You just have to take the first step and actually search for and find the various books, live seminars, home-study DVD courses, speakers, or trainers that resonate with you.

Here are some of the core areas that I have goals in:

- Financial
- Career

- Spirituality
- Mental
- Social/Community
- Family Life
- Physical
- Personal Development

What do I want? What will I achieve? By when will I achieve it? Who are the people I want to meet? What places do I want to travel to? I have a list of over a thousand different goals. Think of it as your *Mise en Place* list!

Step 2. For each goal you have, develop a purpose. Your *why*. Why do you want to achieve that particular goal? If one of your goals is to increase your monthly income, what's the purpose? What's the *why*? Is it so your spouse can quit that job and finally stay home with the kids? Is it so you can move to a neighborhood that's in the best school district in town? Perhaps you want to buy that hot, sexy sports car that you've been dreaming of since you were a teenager. Maybe it's because you haven't put any money away for college yet and one of your kids is going to be applying to schools in the near future. Or is it that you wish to be able to travel with your friends, family, or loved ones on that dream vacation? Whatever your reason, having a strong enough *why* will ignite your passion for making it come true.

Step 3. Seek help from others. This is a crucial step. List others who can help you achieve your goals. Harness the power of networking. Who has already achieved this goal and can teach me something? Or who has the contacts or access to a mentor who has done this? You'll cut your learning curve in half. Not only that, this activity opens doors for you that you may not even have known were there. Learn from others.

Step 4. Make your plan. Ask yourself what steps you must take to achieve your goal. Envision in your mind's eye what the end goal looks like. Break the goal down into a series of actions and tasks that you must complete to achieve your goal. There's a terrific book on the subject from a professor named Stan Davis who taught at Harvard Business School. It's called *Future Perfect*. In the book, he teaches the principle of fast-forward planning by putting yourself at the end of your achievement.

You visualize yourself and look backward to see what steps were involved. For example, think back to your first real kitchen job. Something inside you, unconsciously or consciously, made you realize that you wanted to be in the back of the house, working at that particular place. The sights, the sounds, the uniform—they all made your eyes light up when you first walked into that magical joint. You were either scared witless or as giddy as a teenager about to make it to third base on your first car date, or possibly both. Well, how did you get there? You probably created a plan for how to get an interview and get hired. You saw yourself working there and then did everything you could to figure how to get hired. Maybe you thought about who the chef was that you needed to talk to. You may even have role-played interview questions with family or friends to make sure you didn't become tongue-tied during the conversation. You brushed up on your culinary knowledge by reading the latest cookbooks, and you even bought a new shirt to wear to the interview. See where I'm going here? In the past when you desired an outcome, you naturally tended to organize things that needed to take place in a logical, relevant order to achieve the outcome that you desired. Plan from the end result. It's exciting!

Step 5. Think of the obstacles that will come up, and the solutions to them. According to Sun Tzu, every battle is won before it is ever fought. What roadblocks will arise, and how will you overcome them?

Step 6. TAKE ACTION NOW! What steps will you take immediately? It has been proved over and over that once you have written down a goal and committed to it, one of the best ways to achieve that goal is to do something immediately toward it. No matter how small or how large the goal, do something that will help you achieve it. Let's say you have a goal to lose weight. Immediately after you write out your specific goal (lose 10 pounds) and the time in which you want to achieve it (45 days), you immediately do something toward its completion. You could going for a run or take a half-hour walk, or clean out the refrigerator and pantry of all the junk food. You don't wait until tomorrow to begin accomplishing your goal. No! You do something NOW to help you build momentum. Momentum is power. Work your plan.

Step 7. Evaluate your progress and make necessary adjustments. Ask yourself regularly whether you are on the right path. Then listen. Feedback is crucial to your success. Along your journey, you need to check in and evaluate how things are going. Depending on your tasks and your goals, check-ins could be once a day, once a week, or once a month. There is no right or wrong answer. You have to decide for yourself; it all depends on the task at hand. For example, if I'm building a new restaurant and the process is going to take six months, I won't be asking the general contractor for updates three times a day. That's not realistic. But a weekly check-in to make sure we're on time and on budget would probably make sense and be valuable to everyone. These check-ins shouldn't be too complicated or take up too much time in your already busy schedule. A quick snapshot of what got accomplished since the last check-in, a discussion of any setbacks or problem areas, and an update on how things are progressing against the timeline— that's all you need.

Review this list for a few minutes in the morning and a few minutes in the afternoon or evening. By doing this, you will set your subconscious mind in motion to help you seek out and achieve what you desire. Set realistic goals, and also set some outrageous, *WOW!* goals. Do this for twenty-one days, and watch it become a habit.

Choose to Invest in Yourself

You are an amazing creation! Most of us have no problem singing the praises of others, but we sometimes find it awkward or embarrassing to toot our own horn. That same thinking is what can sometimes make us feel bad about spending money on ourselves personally.

When it comes to your personal development, you need to look at any monies you dedicate to this development as an investment in you. You aren't spending money on books, DVDs, seminars, coaches, mentors and workshops—you're *investing* in those things. And it's an investment that will pay dividends for the rest of your life.

Choose Transformation Truths

When you develop a success mind-set and compose your goals, the following truths will help you evaluate how you are progressing. This becomes the measuring stick.

- You are truly moving forward, or you aren't. What are the obstacles preventing you from moving forward fast?
- You are doing work you truly enjoy, or you aren't. If you don't love, love, *love* what you're doing, others will sense that lack of energy and passion, and your projects will be short-lived.
- You are truly being yourself, or you aren't.
- Your relationships are truly supporting you, or they aren't.
- You truly believe in yourself, or you don't.
- You are truly vibrant and fit, or you aren't.
- You are building wealth, or you're depleting it.
- You are truly stepping up, or you're backing down.
- You are truly mastering something, or you're dabbling. Learn it, do it, master it, and then go do it exceptionally well.

Key Ingredients in Your Recipe for Success

- Key Ingredients in Your Recipe for Success
- Choose your thoughts carefully.
- E + R = O
- Be a goal *doer,* not a goal setter.
- Invest in your education, and invest in yourself. You're worth it!

CHAPTER 11

EVERYTHING IN ITS PLACE

"A man who is careful with his palate is not likely to be careless with his paragraphs."

—Clifton Fadiman

Roll with the Changes and Be Ready to Adapt

One of the biggest threats to building your brand and moving your business forward in this fast-changing marketplace is the unwillingness to embrace and adapt to change. You are going to have to be ready to admit and accept when you make a mistake or pursue a business strategy that may no longer be relevant.

You must also be willing to look ahead and evaluate things that may hurt your business. The world marketplace in general, and the online revolution in particular, are evolving at such a dizzying pace, those who don't practice some "future perfect" planning are going to find themselves left in the dust. Countless brands, products, services, and companies that dominated just a few short years ago are nowhere to be found. You have to be ready to identify opportunities and make adjustments when the landscape changes.

You would be surprised to learn how many large corporations, as well as entrepreneurs, are not very good at identifying or adapting to changing environments. Whether the cause of this is ego, tunnel vision, or just plain shortsightedness, I don't know. But I *can* give you example after example of business owners, brand managers, and entrepreneurs who simply won't achieve their full potential until they embrace a culture of constant change in the marketplace.

Want a real-life example of a brand that let ego get in the way of its positioning? You've probably heard of Cristal Champagne. It is one of the few ultra-luxury brands whose product actually lives up to its hype. I love the stuff!

In the mid- to late 1990s, when hip-hop was reaching its apex in popular music and culture in this country, many of the artists prominently displayed the product in their videos and included numerous references to it in their lyrics. Other luxury brands, such as Gucci, Louis Vuitton, Prada, Maserati, Bentley, and many others, were also benefiting from the FREE exposure that these artists were giving their companies and associated brands.

Cristal was the only company that refused to embrace—and, more importantly, *leverage*—this marketing powerhouse. One of its corporate officers stated in an interview with a mainstream publication that the company wanted to distance itself from the artists and their fans (*millions* of them, by the way). I think the general comment he made was that Cristal couldn't forbid people from buying its product if they were legally able to purchase alcoholic beverages, but that Dom Perignon and Krug would be happy to have their business.

This company had the chance to cultivate and capture major market share with a demographically diverse, powerful, and sustained audience that now touches just about EVERY market in some way, shape, or form. Millions in revenue came knocking at its corporate door, and it said "no thank you." How moronically shortsighted is *that*!

The Rock Star Chef Million Dollar Recipe

Whenever I tell people that they can build their culinary empire, make some bank AND help make the world a better place at the same time by creating their Rock Star Chef brand, they often look at me as though I have two heads. When I share with them that they can get their brands, products or services out there in the marketplace and actually get paid for their expertise, knowledge and culinary POV, most of them look at me as if to say, "Whatever dude…Show me the money –where does all of the cash come from that these 'Rock Star Chefs' make?"

I've gotten that look and that exact question enough times now to know that it's important for me to discuss the money aspect of this business with you. As a bonus for those of you who have read through this book up to this point, I'll do that with you here in this chapter, but please allow me to make a few points before diving into the dollars.

First, I'm a lot like many of my readers and I didn't get into the culinary world with money as the sole focus of my activities. Our craft, the artistry and the history of those who have come before us keep me very humble. The truth is that I am much more driven by sharing what I have learned than by having the ability to purchase any car, house or whatever. Most of that mindset comes from my upbringing. I was raised in an upper middle-class house with two professional working parents who were passionate about their careers and building memories together as a family. While we lived a very comfortable life, traveled the world, took many vacations and never felt a lack for anything. Money and the accumulation of toys wasn't a top priority. Yes we had new cars, motorcycles and a modest boat that we used on vacations and fishing trips, but both my parents instilled in me that money can't buy happiness and one could always judge the character of a man or woman, not by their status, but by their deeds.

However, I have learned some very important lessons about money and wealth over the past few years. Money is an incredible amplifier. If money and wealth are used in proper context, relevant and lasting change can occur. Money will sustain a message, a movement or a cause over the long haul. If money and wealth are put into their proper place, great things can be achieved.

That's why, in this chapter, I'm going to be frank and upfront about money and how it's made in our industry. I'm trying to save you from being another wanna-be Rock Star Chef whose message or business was a one-hit wonder or worse…one that never got out of the starting gate.

Alright, let's get rockin'… How exactly can chefs, restaurateurs and culinary entrepreneurs make money in the New Digital Economy? How could you make a million dollars without having to create massive overhead that stifles your entrepreneurial freedom? Almost every product, program or service that I am going to show you here falls into one of four buckets. My job is to get you exposed and trained in this whole new world of digital marketing. Yes, there's a TON of people selling food online. But that's not what this is about. If you want to learn how to do that or if you are currently selling your branded products in the marketplace, we teach you how to amplify those sales at our Rock Star Chef Marketing Academy.

Now, I know that you see tons of chefs or restaurants or various brands selling soup, sauces, jams, jellies, oils, vinegars, spices, spice rubs, marinades, smoked salmon, flavored butters and many other items online. As you know from my story, that's exactly what I did back in the day when I first started learning how to market gourmet food products in stores and on the web, but allow me to expose you to some products, programs and services that are consumed by your customers in a different way. What I mean is that besides just consuming your food or recipes…your customers might also consume your offerings by reading something, watching something, hearing something or experiencing something live that you created. Thanks to THIS specific point in human history that we are now blessed to live in…it's much, much easier that you would have ever imagined.

Seven Master Ingredients For Rock Star Chefs
Rock Star Chefs can make money through one or more of the following activities:

- Writing
- Speaking
- Doing Live Events (Pop-ups, cruises, guest appearances, food shows, etc.)
- Consulting (recipe development, opening chef, culinary spokesperson, etc.)
- Coaching/Teaching (Sushi classes, BBQ training, Baking & Pastry classes, etc.)
- Travel (Wine tours, working farms, food centric travel or exploration)
- Online Marketing

As an author, Rock Star Chefs share their knowledge or expertise in a certain area of the culinary world and charge money for it. This can be a traditional how-to cookbook, or a memoir like *Kitchen Confidential*. While writing a traditional cookbook is the most common form of monetizing writing for chefs and culinary professionals, there are also many other options. My clients and I have made money selling e-books (shorter electronic versions of book, often 20-60 pages in length), instructor guides, mobile apps, private membership sites (which people paid a subscription fee to read and could access with a unique login and password), specialized articles series and monthly subscription newsletters (delivered both in print to my customers' home and electronically to their email address once a month for a fee).

As speakers, presenters or culinary ambassadors, Rock Star Chefs make money by delivering content and presentations on their culinary expertise in one of three formats. First, they may position and market themselves as speakers, charging organizations a speaking fee for what is typically a 30 to 90 minute speech. Second, when judging a culinary competition or acting as a host/MC for an event, one can charge a significant daily rate for being a part of events like this. Finally, many corporations or brands (CPG companies) will often seek to hire culinary talent to be their Brand Ambassador or Culinary Spokesperson for one of their campaigns. If the campaign is successful, this can turn into a long and lucrative gig.

Live events can be a great way to earn income and quickly build your brand out in the marketplace. Matter of fact, it's my belief that live events are often the most lucrative activity for entrepreneurial chefs. Social media is a perfect platform for these types of events because they are so in the moment and people love to share an event like this. They are also one of the greatest positioning tools you have. A savvy Rock Star Chef could generate millions of dollars in free publicity with just one live event.

As consultants, Rock Star Chefs make money by charging companies and individuals, usually by the hour or by the completed project, for their actual services in creating, collaborating on, and completing a specific project. One could also structure a deal so as to earn royalties on any work created. (Just like royalties on music that is created by musicians). Everyday there are thousands of chefs and culinary professionals around the world who are working away in kitchens and boardrooms creating recipes, new restaurants, new ingredient combinations and thousands of other ideas all centered around food. This was where I first got started in this side of the business, outside of working in a traditional kitchen.

Coaching/Teaching/Travel—I group all of these together because at their core, they revolve around taking your expertise, your passions or your experiences and monetizing them in different and unique ways. I will give a few examples of each, but really the possibilities are endless because there is so much interest in food right now in our culture. People often seek coaching in pursuit of improving an area of their personal or professional life. Many of the professional chefs who compete in culinary competitions often seek out previous winners of these events to "coach" them on how to have an edge during the event. Some chefs I know have traveled to Italy to work in famous wineries; pizza shops, charcuterie or even pasta manufacturers to learn how to improve their skills back home.

One of my O.G. Rock Star Chef friends from back in the day made a fortune teaching sushi making technique and skills to the Park Avenue crowd in New York City back in the mid-90's when the trend was becoming popular in the city. Another colleague of mine and his wife set up private VIP winery tours throughout Europe at many of the premier legacy vineyards and estates. They charge tens of thousands of dollars per couple for a 10-day experience and travel in first-class luxury the entire time. They do this about 2-3 times per year. Finally, one of my Texas buddies teaches a 3-Day course on Texas BBQ to professionals who travel from all over the world to attend his classes. He is sold out six months in advance and has a waiting list for cancellations. He works about 6 months out of the year and takes the rest of the year off to spend with family, go hunting, drink beer, etc.

Finally, as online marketers, Rock Star Chefs make money by packaging their knowledge and culinary expertise into products, programs and services that people purchase online. This is the new "Holy

Grail" for chefs and all entrepreneurs. The web and almost ubiquitous access to a high speed Internet has laid waste to old distribution models and allowed us to instantly communicate with, and sell to our customers all over the world. Rock Star Chefs can now offer their content, expertise or how-to training through webinars, membership sites, downloadable audio and video programs, monthly exclusive content releases, desktop training programs and hundreds of other concepts. Today's Rock Star Chefs are essentially online retailers of information and how-to expertise. And unlike our brick-and-mortar counterparts, our business is BOOMING! Setting up a digital presence is faster, cheaper and easier than ever. At Rock Star Chef Marketing Academy, we've shown and proved how entrepreneurial chefs can be up and running online in less than a day. It's truly incredible.

The awesome part about all of these roles is that you get to choose which best matches your personality and lifestyle preference. You can choose whether or not you work out of your home or another location. You can choose to travel or stay close to home. You can work one-on-one as a consultant or you can present to many up on stage and under the lights.

While choice is certainly wonderful, you can also choose not to make a choice (wasn't that a Rush song lyric?). Most Rock Star Chefs, at least those of us who are building seven-figure businesses and culinary empires, choose to play many of these roles as part of our business strategy. The truth is that if you only play one of these roles, you are essentially limiting your income and you might be in danger of creating a business that isn't sustainable.

Here's a very common example. A few of the people who have attended Rock Star Chef Marketing Academy have been Amazon and *New York Times* best-selling authors. Many people think that these authors were beyond wealthy and famous. The harsh reality is that a few are unknown and broke. How can that be possible? Because though they had a best-selling book, there was nothing beyond the book—they didn't have a backend product funnel. There was no additional product or service or special event that was available for customers to purchase. Most of them didn't have a website or any kind of digital presence that captured names and email addresses. When their 15 minutes of fame was over, their new fans had nothing else to purchase. This story is so commonplace, and not just for cookbook authors by the way, many authors share the same story of misery. I can think of no other industry that rivals the number of one-hit wonders in its marketplace except for the music industry.

To truly evolve and grow as a Rock Star Chef, you will want to begin building expertise and success in all seven areas into a multiple-streams-of income business model. Now there's no hard and fast rule that says you have to do this, but trust me, once you have had success in one or more areas and see the results that you can achieve…You-Will-Want-To-Do-This!

I'm a best-selling author, an in-demand speaker, a coach with a waiting list of clients, a business consultant who gets to pick and choose only the best clients and projects to work with and an online marketer responsible for millions of dollars in revenue. Now, here is the best part: I and blessed to be able to do this with minimal staff and an extremely simple business model. That last point is worth repeating. As an entrepreneur in the New Digital Economy, you don't need a large staff or huge overhead. How is this possible? It's possible because in most cases, all the infrastructure you need in this business is a phone, a laptop, a high-speed internet connection, a way to process payments from customers, a decent video camera and a culinary message for POV that you wish to share with the world. From there, most all of your activities are going to be based around strategic branding, positioning, marketing and partnering with others to build your culinary empire.

Step-by-Step Method For A Million Dollar Culinary Empire

Let me show you how all of these roles and profit centers can come together to create a very simple, yet highly strategic plan for building a million-dollar Rock Star Chef business.

This plan was created for one of my high-dollar coaching clients, who asked me once, very direct and bluntly, "Mark, I need you to develop me a plan to make a million dollars in twelve months, and I want to be able to do it without having to build out another huge infrastructure like I currently have or relying on 'chalk-talk' to creating tens of thousands of new clients."

In almost every aspect of our current culinary world this would an almost impossible task. Think about it for a minute, could you create a business from scratch right now, today that could generate almost $100,000 per month in revenue, with huge profit margins on low-to-no overhead or infrastructure? Could you accomplish this without any heavy capital investment in raw materials, production capabilities or a sales team? In the New Digital Economy, this type of scenario is pretty straightforward. In fact, I showed the client that he could accomplish his goal with just hundreds of customers, with limited staff and by following the Now do you understand why I scream from the roof tops that we live in an incredible moment in human history that is ripe with opportunity?

I've created an exclusive video presentation for you that goes into extreme, step-by-step detail of the exact plan with number of units, total revenue, etc. that I created for that coaching client I told you about earlier. You can view the most up to date version of the Million Dollar Recipe over at www.RockStarChef.com/milliondollarplan.

It's All on You

Throughout this book are many timeless messages and themes that can revolutionize your work, your brand, and your life. In the end, though, your success—or the lack of it—is entirely up to you! Read that last line again and let it soak in, even though it can sound a little scary. Never before in the history of marketing and business has the playing field been so level for almost all the players.

With some of the tools, platforms, tips, and techniques I've shared with you in this book, (including the million dollar recipe) it is now possible for a PASSIONATE individual to create a successful business, product line, or brand that can compete with *any* Fortune 500 company and its multimillion-dollar advertising budget. The tools that are available online can spread your ideas and personal brand further, faster, and for far less money than ever before…but these tools are only as effective as the Rock Star Chef wielding them.

Trust Your Inner Chef: You Are a Maverick

You and I have just been on quite a journey together. Throughout this book, I hope I have made you feel inspired, motivated, and educated on how you can dramatically improve your personal and professional life. You have a unique fund of knowledge and experience that you can and *must* share with the world! Oh, and by the way, you can be paid for that knowledge and make a difference in your financial life as well. You can begin or advance in your journey to becoming a Rock Star Chef simply by learning to intelligently and strategically position, promote, and package your brand, products, or services.

Listen to the inner voice inside you that knows how incredible you are. You have the tools to begin serving others and reaching a deep personal fulfillment that you may have always longed for. In the end, this is not just a business book. Nor is it a tell-all "behind the kitchen door" book. And it's not one of those dry, boring how-to books that make you feel as if you were sitting in a classroom when you're reading it. That's not what I'm after here.

What I hope to have accomplished with this book is to reach out to all my colleagues in the industry, whatever their current level of success or experience, and help them get a leg up with their career or their business.

This is a book for chefs who have already established themselves as household names. It's also for the men and women who are just starting out their journey in this crazy life we call culinary arts. More than anything else, this is a book meant to remind readers that with the tools and strategies discussed in this book, they can and will prosper in this New Digital Economy. Life and technology are changing our business lives at a frantic pace. Trying to decide where to market and engage with consumers on all these new digital platforms can seem overwhelming. It can also be daunting to try to figure out where to learn best practices for growing your business in a meaningful way.

And, maybe more than anything else, it can be tough to figure out whom to trust for strategic advice and proven marketing campaigns. It is my humble wish that you view me as a trusted source for advice on intelligent positioning and best practices of what is working now in the new economy, as well as the step-by-step recipe for how to execute it all.

Mise en Place Revealed

"Mise en Place is the religion of all great line cooks."
—Anthony Bourdain

If you've read this far, then you know more about how to package, position, and promote yourself as a Rock Star Chef than I did when I began. I have been blessed with personal and professional success as a result of these concepts, and I am EAGER to hear what you do with this info. You've got a great foundation and understanding of the basics, which will give you a head start on the next generation of Rock Star Chefs.

In fact, I'd be willing to bet money that you probably know more about this segment of our industry than most celebrity chefs who are out on the circuit today, because until now very few (if any) of those who knew shared their best practices and methods. I just ask that when you come in contact with up-and-coming or struggling chefs and restaurateurs on your tour, lend them a helping hand.

Ours has always been an industry in which we share, nurture, and collectively take under our wing the newbies coming into the culinary world. I can't think of another industry where the apprentice/mentor relationship is as alive and thriving as in the culinary world. Let's make sure we continue to honor the masters who came before us and who originally helped us along our path.

I'm not sure what combination of traits, influences, and happenstance has you reading my words and thoughts at this moment, but I must tell you, I feel honored and humbled that our paths have crossed and that you have given me the opportunity to share with you what I have learned. To this day, I am still a student and constantly learning. True Rock Star Chefs are always learning and never lose their thirst for knowledge. They also instinctively know to keep their egos in check—well, okay, **most** of them!

It's been great fun writing this book for you and our culinary community. Having had the privilege of working with thousands of chefs, restaurateurs, and food service experts from around the world, I believe I have a gut feeling about why you've been reading this book and have found my message at this point in your career and life. It is my belief that deep down inside you is a restless stirring that you have long felt, urging you to share your voice with the world in a bigger way.

Maybe you picked up this book because you saw another chef or restaurateur sharing their life story or experience with others, and you realized that you wanted to do the same thing. Or maybe you're someone who is already on the path to becoming a Rock Star Chef, and you were looking for new ideas, strategies, and best practices to amplify and accelerate your career more loudly, broadly, and profitably. Either way, I believe that your being here is proof that your message has a place in this world and that we all will be better served by it.

If you are one of the clever readers of this book (and aren't all Rock Star Chefs clever?) you may have noticed that name of each chapter begins with the letters that form the ubiquitous French culinary term "*Mise en Place.*"

It loosely means "everything in its place." In the kitchen brigade, all your prep work, your station, and your tools could fall under this term. Before you begin any recipe production, you gather or create your *Mise en Place* so that you can efficiently produce your masterpiece. As a cook, your station, and its condition—it's state of readiness, is an extension of you and your nervous system. The culinary gods and the culinary universe are all in alignment when your station is set up properly and efficiently. Many of you know what I'm talking about…you know where to find everything on your station with your eyes closed. You don't even have to think about where everything to cook with is on your station. You, your station, and your mise are all one with each other as you dance through the evenings rush without pause. On your way to becoming a Rock Star Chef, the process is the same.

Allow me to explain:

- **M**ind-Set
- **I**ntegrity
- **S**alesmanship
- **E**xercise
- **E**fficiency

- Networking
- Promote
- Like-Minded Individuals
- Always Give Back
- Choices
- Everything in Its Place

Those are the chapters that make up this book, and if you follow the process, you are well on your way to becoming a Rock Star Chef.

In his new book, *Work Clean*, author Dan Charnas argues that chefs are the **ultimate** productivity gurus thanks to Mise en Place. During a recent interview with Food & Wine magazine, these were his words that explained that compliment in the most sophisticated, concise and elegant way possible:

"Oh my God, it's so elegant, this system. It's not just about organizing space, it's actually about how you relate to space, how you relate to time, how you relate to motions within that space, how you relate to managing resources, how you relate to managing people, how you relate to managing your personal energies, all of that. For whatever ironic reason, those spiritual wisdoms have fallen to the chefs. It sounds bizarre, but the fact of the matter is the reason that chefs have done it and lawyers have not, or that chefs have done it and medical doctors have not, is that the chef has a particular set of restraints and circumstances that make it impossible for him to succeed without doing this kind of planning of time, space, motion, resources and people."

If you were already familiar with the term, can you now relate to the thinking and process behind my message? Starting today, you have the recipe, plan, system, or whatever you want to call it to begin your journey to becoming a Rock Star Chef. At the end of each chapter is a checklist for you to use, to make sure you GET THINGS DONE. It may seem simple, but so often, the profoundest things are.

I don't think you would begin prepping for a five-hundred-person, five-course sit-down banquet menu by just winging it! No, for something so involved, you would have prep lists, to-do lists, order guides, calendar of events, staffing schedule, and hourly detail, just for starters. So …why would you think that mapping out a strategic plan for your business goals and dreams would require any less attention?

Now that you hold in your head and in your hands the knowledge that I've shared with you in this book, do something with it! *Please,* put it into action! Don't let this just become a rah-rah feel-good message that you read once and put on the bookshelf. The unfortunate truth is, I know that the final barrier to getting started and staying the course is one that prevents most people from realizing their dreams. That barrier is always the same: fear.

When it comes right down to it, you may be afraid that no one will listen to your message, visit your restaurant, or buy your products. Or maybe you're worried that corporate sponsors won't find you credible enough to represent their brands. You may also be afraid that if you build out the various social media platforms that center on you, your brand, or your services, no one will interact with your pages.

May I share something with you? They will! Customers are people, and all people have the same desire: they want value. And when you give them your best they will support you, buy from you, and brag about you to their friends—and they will even *envy* you a little.

Let's face it: our industry is pretty exciting and glamorous to the rest of the world. The popularity of food, cooking, and chefs is strong, and I don't think that will pass anytime soon. What we do is seen as an art form as well as a lifestyle.

Take comfort in the fact that in almost every part of the world, when you mention that you are a chef or are in the restaurant business, everyone can relate to what you do, and everyone has some fond memory of food or a special meal that happened in their lives.

I hope that in writing *How to Become a Rock Star Chef,* I have become a fond memory for you, and a part of your story. As our world and society continue to change and evolve, people are increasingly overwhelmed and unsure how to react to all that is happening in their personal and professional lives. They are looking for solutions and a calming voice in the storm of chaos. When you seek to add value to their lives in some small way, they will reward you with their business and loyalty.

Be the Rock Star Chef who does more than anyone else to outserve your guests and potential customers. Not only will this make you stand out from the competition, you will quickly find that *there is no competition*!

See you soon, Rock Star Chef.

—**Mark**

ACKNOWLEDGMENTS

I continue to count my blessings every day for the successes I've had, and this always reminds me of just how lucky I am for all the life experiences that I've had up to this point. Let's face it, though. Not one of us attains any level of achievement without the help, guidance, and support of others. One of our greatest experiences as human beings is the way that our interactions with others help shape our thoughts, habits, dreams, and goals. That the people who come in and out of our lives affect who we are and who we become by the lessons they teach us is nothing short of magical.

Countless mentors, friends, coaches, family members, bosses, colleagues, and complete strangers have influenced the person that I have become and the way I view the world. There is not enough room on the pages that follow to acknowledge them all, but I want to try by giving special thanks to at least a few.

This book is dedicated to my mom and dad, Johanna and Gino. Without your love, guidance, and support, I would never have had the marvelous life that I have. I hope I have lived up to the dreams and vision you both had on that December night so long ago.

To my sweet baby girl Alexis, words are poor tools to express the immense love, pride and devotion I feel toward you. You have made me strive to be a better man and have brightened every day of my life since you came into it. Just a few days after you were born, an old friend told me, "*A daddy will never know a greater love than that of his daughter.*" Each day, in your own special way, you make those words come to life, and I cherish you for it.

To the group of buddies who have stayed in touch all these years despite my crazy travel schedule and through all of life's adventures, I honor you. For your lifelong friendship, I love you: Marc McDowell, Elton Reid, Jay Bomgaars and James Sanchez.

To the first real Rock Star Chef I ever met in my life, Jean Louis Toussaint from Comme Chez Vous. If not for you, I would never have developed a love for my heritage embraced through food. Your passion for simple ingredients, expertly prepared with refinement and respect, is still a cornerstone of my cooking today.

To my mentors, bosses, colleagues, friends, and coworkers at the various companies I've had the privilege to work with, I appreciate all the business lessons, professionalism, and all-around excellence that you've shared with me. Thanks especially to Chef Tom Keller, Chef Mark Erickson, Chef Victor Gielisse, Chef David Kellaway, Chef Mo Kanner, Chef Paul Sartory, Chef Tom Keith, Chef Vince Fatigati, Chef Dave Kamen, Chef/President Tim Ryan, Phil Papineau, Chef Andre Diddy, Danny Wegman, Tony Tedesco, Gianfranco DiCarlo, Cliff Smith, Phil Romano, Girard Lewis, John Campbell, Fully Clingman, Charles Butt, Red McCombs, Ella Brennan, Charles Redfield, Jonathan Weis, Al Baldacci, Chef Kevan Vetter, Chef Len King, Chef Gary Patterson, Chef Gabby Quintana, Merri Kingsley, Lori Robinson, Ken Stickevers, Jill Pratt, Jen LaFrance, Mary-Beth Harington, Alan Wilson, Martha Stewart, Tim Ferriss and of course Barry Wacksman.

Very special thanks to Scott Hoffman, Über agent and a serious Rock Star in his own right! I appreciate your candid advice, publishing perspective, mixology enthusiasm and literary wisdom. Not to mention, you are a serious foodie in your own right—that amazing meal at Eleven Madison Park will go down in history as one of the best meals I have ever had.

My friend, mentor and coach Brendon Burchard deserves huge credit here for guiding me through this journey. Without your wisdom, instruction, and confidence, this book would still be a pipe dream. I'm here…Thank you, Brendon, for everything.

To my amazing Center Ring family, you guys rock! I value each of you for our incredible journey together now, and in the future: Carlos Marin, Nikki Nitz, Camper Bull, Jefferson Santos, Mikell Parsons, Cecy Marin, JJ Virgin, Marcelle Pick, Alan Ting, Susanne Bennett, Billie Thompson, Lori Lee Barr, Jan Lorentzen, Lisa Scolnick, Micki Aronson, Wayne Pernell, Jose Gomez, Alan Christianson, Todd Johnson, Deri Llewellyn-Davies, Wolfgang Payne, Jose Gomez, Stefan Gratziani, Krystelle Gratziani, Jennifer Landa, Joe Tatta, Krisstina Wise, David Gottfried, Joan Rosenberg, Kimberly Faith Jones, Sara Gottfried, Gry Sinding, Mel Abraham, Marty Scirratt, Jenni Robbins, and Molly Curran.

To my new family at Avocados From Mexico; Alvaro Luque (El Presidente), Stephanie Browder (my partner in crime), Stephanie Bazan, Kevin Hamilton, Maggie Bezart, Anna Kirsch, Ivonne Kinser, Alejandro Duran, Sofia Ibarguengoytia, Anna Mertz, Miguel Molina, Esmeralda Blanco, Alfonso Delgado, Diane Le, Tanya Edwards, Grisel Perez, Oscar Garcia, Ryan Fukuda, Esmeralda Blanco, Dunia Alguero, Eric Coronado, Mike Brown, Ron Campbell, Ricardo Javier Vega Lopez, Ramon Paz, Armando Lopez Orduna, Martin and the entire Board of Directors. Special shout out to Patti Jinich and Maggie Jimenez. I thank you for the inspired journey we are on and for all of your support, guidance and friendship. For my new friends and colleagues at Ketchum; Amy Shipley, Steve Siegelman, Gabby Lovelace, Amy Austin, Julie Willbrand and at Augustine Ideas; Robert Nelson, Jill Bilby, Alessandra Bottini and Angelo Nelson—You Guys Rock! Thanks for all of the tireless hours and creative insight to our many projects.

To the webmaster, digital creative, great friend and all-around rock star himself; Kristian Bottini is the brains and creative genius behind everything associated with ROCKSTARCHEF online. Could not have done this without you brother!

There have been some truly amazing women along life's journey whom I've had the privilege, blessing and honor of knowing and sharing life's beautiful memories with: Lisa, Elyse, Cari Jo, and Tansy... you have influenced me and this book in so many ways through your grace, love of life, servant hearts and especially your unique view of the world... thank you.

AUTHOR'S NOTE: E-MAIL ME

I wrote this book as a response to the avalanche of requests from friends, colleagues, mentors and enjoyable others wanting to know exactly what I was doing in my business and in my clients businesses online that was generating so much success. There's so much bullshit advice out in the marketplace about Digital Marketing, Social Media and Mobile that it's hard to separate the experts from the poseurs. I have a saying that I share with clients and colleagues; *"If someone tells you they are an expert or guru in this space, RUN - because the world of digital is changing rapidly and what once worked yesterday no longer works today"*. Platforms fall in and out of favor weekly and to have any kind of relevant success, one must be a constant student of this space and always be testing, implementing and learning best practices.

I believe that the more you engage, instruct and inspire your customers, the more you will dominate your market and the competition. If you create marketing that people genuinely want and don't hop on the digital marketing "flavor of the month" bandwagon and instead focus on solving problems, answering questions and building long-lasting relationships with your customers…then you will realize you don't *have* any competition.

You and your business are being forced to compete for your customers' attention against their family members, best friends and circles of influence. If you're consistently relevant and useful to your customers and if you commit to inform rather than promote, those customers will reward you and your business with trust, loyalty and their dollars.

Continue the Conversation and Win Cool Prizes at RockStarChefBook.com

This isn't the end of your Rock Star Chef journey; it's just the beginning. Much like a young apprentice or a beginner musician, the path to becoming a master chef or a virtuoso constantly grows and expands. I'll be right there with you on this journey and I want to celebrate and chronicle your success stories and share with you best practices at the official website RockStarChef.com. This is where you will find resources to help you along your path. I invite you to visit right now and see what's available.

Photo Contest

Take a photo of the book "In The Wild" and post it to Twitter with the hashtag #RockStarChefRules and you could win amazing prizes and unlock bonus content. All the details are at RockStarChefBook.com

Rock Star Chef Training In Your Company

If you're interested in discovering how you can apply the Rock Star Chef recipe in your own company, through my consulting firm, I conduct audits and custom design programs with people like you to create truly useful and measurable marketing.

Rock Star Chef Live

Lastly, if you think your company, customers or students would be inspired by the Rock Star Chef message, let me know. I'm on the road often, presenting to corporate and conference audiences, showing people how smart marketing in the digital age is about strategic positioning and intelligent campaigning.

I sincerely hope you enjoyed this book. Most of all, I hope you found it useful and that you will implement what you have learned into your work. I'd love to talk about the book, answer any questions you may have and stay connected. E-mail me at mark@chefmarkgarcia.com.

Will You Do Me A Solid?

If you enjoyed *How To Become a Rock Star Chef,* would you mind taking a minute to write a review on Amazon? Positive or negative doesn't matter, I just ask that you be honest so that your review will help others decide if this book will help them on their journey—Thanks!

ABOUT THE AUTHOR

 Chef Mark Garcia is the founder of Rock Star Chef Marketing Academy and best selling co-author of *Entrepreneurial Insanity in the Restaurant Business.* He is one of the top culinary innovators and digital strategists in the country.

Mark is a digital native of the social and commercial Web. His digital prowess began in the late 1990s, when he learned to sell goods and services online as well as build Web presence for some of the nation's largest food retailers. Many celebrity chefs such as Wolfgang Puck, Guy Fieri, Gordon Ramsay, and John Besh have benefited from his expertise in strategic marketing, recipe development, and retail merchandising. Due to these successes, he has dedicated his life to helping culinary artists and organizations find their voice, establish their presence online, and engage their community with greater impact.

Chef Mark's videos, newsletters, recipes, and appearances inspire millions of people each year. He is often quoted in the media about food trends and the constantly evolving world of food here in the United

States and in the global marketplace. Outlets such as CNN, NBC News, BBC, Nation's Restaurant News, Flavor & The Menu, Plate Magazine, HispanicBusiness.com, Forbes.com, Smithsonian.com, and WSJ.com have all featured him.

As one of the most in-demand trainers of our time, Mark has shared the stage with Brian Solis, Eric Ripert, Tim Ferris, Dr. Oz, and Deepak Chopra. In the digital thought leader space, Mark has shared presentations and workshops with executives from LinkedIn, Google, Yahoo, Adobe, Cisco, and R/GA. *Fast Company* magazine name him "one of the most influential persons online." His clients have included some of the largest companies in the world, as well as entrepreneurs and executives from all facets of the restaurant, manufacturing, hospitality, and retail industries.

If you've ever eaten out at a restaurant or bought a meal inside a grocery store or dined at a destination hotel while on vacation, there's a good chance he played a role in the food you enjoyed…especially if it was an avocado.

Meet him and receive free training at www.ChefMarkGarcia.com

Morgan James
Speakers Group

⤴ www.TheMorganJamesSpeakersGroup.com

We connect Morgan James published
authors with live and online events
and audiences whom will benefit
from their expertise.

Printed in the USA
CPSIA information can be obtained
at www.ICGtesting.com
JSHW022344140824
68134JS00019B/1675